THE OCEAN WATCHER

Learn to Understand Your Career
Through the Perils of the Sea

ButterflyMan

Publisher:
ButterflyMan Publishing LLC
Website: https://www.butterflyman.com
Contact: contact@butterflyman.com

Printed in the United States of America
ISBN: 979-8-90217-015-0

Directory

Chapter One: Opening Fable 11

Chapter Two: The Beach Walker 15

Chapter Three: The Swimmer.. 19

Chapter Four: The Diver 22

Chapter Five: The Ocean Researcher.. 28

Chapter Six: The Practitioner · The Watcher 36

Chapter Seven: Up, Down, Left, Right — Your Coordinates in the Industry 41

Chapter Eight: Currents and Undercurrents — The Power of Environment 46

Chapter Nine: Creatures of the Ocean_The Humanity and Roles Around You...................... 51

Chapter Ten: Storms and Surprises_How to Face Unpredictable Career Crises 56

Chapter Eleven: Lighthouse and Sea Routes_What Kind of Person Do You Want to Become?... 60

Chapter Twelve: Direction and Destination_The Final Coordinates of Life 65

Chapter Thirteen: Companions and Partings_Who Will Walk with You to the End?............. 70

Chapter Fourteen: Islands and Harbors_The Stopping Points Along the Journey.................. 75

Chapter fifteen: The Stars of Navigation_How to Find Guidance in Darkness...................... 79

Chapter sixteen: The Ocean and the Continent_Career Transitions and Transformation.............. 83

Chapter Seventeen: Companions of the Voyage_The Power of Cooperation and Teamwork....... 88

Chapter Eighteen: Lighthouse and Voyage_Leadership and Legacy...................................... 93

Chapter Nineteen: The Ultimate Trial of Sailing_Solitude and Freedom.............................. 97

Chapter Twenty: Homecoming and Rebirth_After You Have Crossed the Sea.................... 101

Chapter Twenty one: The Sea and the Stars_The Ultimate Meaning of Career 105

Reader's Guide — Your Navigation Manual 112

📖 Dedication

To those still standing on the shore,
may you find the courage to step into the sea and let the waves touch your feet.

To the swimmers struggling in the tides,
may you not only stay afloat, but also discover your true direction.

To the divers descending into the deep,
may you endure the weight of darkness and pressure, and still find hidden light and treasure.

To the researchers who chart the seas,
may your insight and maps become the guiding routes for those who follow.

To the dreamers who gaze at the stars,
may your vision be more than a distant spark—may it become a steady compass.

To the pioneers who dare to land on new continents,
may you face jungles and thorns without fear, and root yourself in new soil to build anew.

And to all who are willing to light the lamp as watchers of the sea,
because of you, others in the dark will find their way home;
because of you, the ocean is no longer mere drifting, but a passage toward hope.

🕊️ Acknowledgments

Writing this book has been a long voyage.
The sea was vast, the land distant, the stars flickered, and storms came without warning.
Along the way, many people lit their lighthouses for me, so that in fog and waves I would not be entirely lost.

I thank the friends who shared their struggles about careers,
your stories became different sea routes that showed me: each of us is searching for our own coordinate on this ocean.

I thank my mentors and colleagues,
you were the islands and harbors of my professional journey,
teaching me that work is not only a way to make a living, but also a path of growth and transformation.

I thank those who stayed with me in storms,
you were the oarsmen who rowed by my side,
reminding me that true courage is not the absence of fear, but the choice to set sail despite fear.

Lastly, I thank the sea and the stars.
The sea reminded me: waves will never stop for anyone, but they forge our resilience.
The stars reminded me: no matter how dark the night, direction still exists—lift your eyes, and you will see the light.

And I thank the lighthouse, which taught me this:
everything we pass through is not only for ourselves,
but to leave behind a flame,
so that those who come after us can still find their way through the dark.

Table of contents :

Chapter 1: Opening Parable
- Why use the ocean as a metaphor for a career?
- A career is like the sea—vast, changing, dangerous, but full of possibilities.
- Everyone must answer: *"Where am I in the ocean?"*

Chapter 2: The One Standing on the Shore
- Characteristic: Hesitant, only watching, afraid to step in.
- Mindset: Fear of risk, comfort in safety, yet longing for the ocean.
- Metaphor: Not yet truly in a career—still on the margins (e.g., just graduated, stuck in low-level jobs).
- Reflection: Are you only "watching others from the shore"?

Chapter 3: The Swimmer
- Already in the water, floating freely, but with limited range.
- Enjoys the fun of the water but lacks direction, easily carried by currents.
- Metaphor: A typical employee—capable but drifting.
- Key point: Learn to set your rhythm and direction, not just "float."

Chapter 4: The Diver
- Dares to go deep, sees what others cannot.
- Mindset: Yearns for depth, but requires skill, tools, and courage.
- Metaphor: A professional with expertise who explores the depths of an industry.
- Challenge: The deeper you dive, the greater the risks—lack of oxygen, hidden currents, predators.
- Reflection: Are you constantly training and equipping yourself to dive deeper?

Chapter 5: The Ocean Researcher

- Not only swims and dives but understands overall patterns.
- Mindset: Explores, records, analyzes, and even proposes new theories.
- Metaphor: Experts, thinkers, leaders who can see the bigger picture of the industry.
- Key point: Researchers don't just *do*—they explain and predict.

Chapter 6: The Practitioner: Becoming a Watcher
- Applies knowledge, both guarding the ocean and guiding others.
- Metaphor: Mentors and leaders who share maps and protect newcomers.
- Philosophy: True growth is not about "conquering the sea" but "living with the sea."

Chapter 7: Your Above, Below, Left, and Right
- Above: The sky—goals and inspiration.
- Below: The seabed—values, roots, and history.
- Left: Fellow travelers—peers, colleagues, competitors.
- Right: The unknown—emerging fields, opportunities, challenges.

Chapter 8: Currents and Undercurrents
- Surface currents: Visible trends (policies, markets, hot industries).
- Deep undercurrents: Invisible forces (culture, relationships, values).
- Storms and accidents: Economic crises, company failures, technological shifts.
- Key: Learn to *read the currents* rather than drift blindly.

Chapter 9: Creatures of the Sea
- Small fish: Beginners, dependent, fast learners.
- Sharks: Predators—aggressive competitors.
- Whales: Giants—big corporations or industry leaders.
- Sea turtles: Long-distance travelers—slow but enduring.
- Coral reefs: Teams and organizational culture.
- Impostors: Beautiful outside but poisonous within.

Chapter 10: Storms and Accidents — Facing Unpredictable Career Crises
- Hurricanes: Global or industry-level disruptions.
- Reefs: Hidden rules and traps in the workplace.
- Fog: Uncertainty and lack of information.
- Coping: Maintain buoyancy (resilience and skills), learn positioning (self-awareness), build a lighthouse (values and direction).

Chapter 11: Lighthouse and Course — What Kind of Person Do You Want to Be?
- Lighthouse: Values, beliefs, direction.
- Course: Career path and choices.
- Three types of people:
1. Without a lighthouse—drifting.
2. With a lighthouse but no course—goals without practice.
3. With both lighthouse and course—true navigators.
- Question: Where is *your* lighthouse?

Chapter 12: Direction and Destination — The Final Coordinates of Life
- A career is not just drifting, but voyaging.
- Destination is not a physical shore, but an inner coordinate.
- Three destinations:
1. Material (salary, position).
2. Spiritual (passion, meaning).
3. Legacy (leaving behind a path for others).

Chapter 13: Companionship and Separation — Who Will Stay Until the End?
- Companions: Friends, peers, colleagues.
- Separation: Some disembark midway, others choose different paths.
- Truth: Most people only accompany you for part of the journey.
- Key: Have you found true companions?

Chapter 14: Islands and Harbors — Temporary Stops Along the Journey
- Meaning: Rest, repair, resupply.
- Types: Learning islands, transformation harbors, healing ports.
- Risk: Comfort makes people stop moving.
- Wisdom: Stops are for new departures, not endings.

Chapter 15: The Stars of Navigation — Finding Guidance in Darkness
- The North Star: Ultimate goal.
- Constellations: Stage-based goals.
- Starlight: Faith and inner strength.
- Insight: Darkness is not scary—as long as you look up, stars are always there.

Chapter 16: Sea and Land — Career Crossovers and Transformations
- Sea: Instability and wandering.
- Land: Rooting and stability.
- Three transitions: Sea to land, land to sea, sea-land balance.

Chapter 17: Companions of the Voyage — Power of Cooperation and Teams
- Three types of companions:
1. Fellow travelers—row beside you.
2. Mentors—light a distant lamp.
3. Followers—grow in your light.
- Team power: Knowledge complementarity, strength accumulation, extended dreams.

Chapter 18: Lighthouse and Voyage — Leadership and Legacy
- Essence of leadership: Not control, but illumination.
- Meaning of a lighthouse: Direction, hope, legacy.
- Four stages of leadership: Ignite yourself, ignite others, stand firm in darkness, leave sparks for the next generation.

Chapter 19: The Ultimate Test — Loneliness and Freedom
- Three levels of loneliness: Physical, emotional, existential.
- Price of freedom: Without loneliness, no true freedom.
- Wisdom: Balance between solitude and liberty.
- Insight: Loneliness makes you yourself; freedom lets you shape the future.

Chapter 20: Return and Renewal — After Crossing the Ocean
- Meaning of return: Reflection, sharing, resupply.
- Renewal: Learning patience, choice, and legacy.
- New call: Return is not the end but a new beginning.

Chapter 21: Ocean and Stars — The Final Meaning of a Career
- The Ocean: Survival and reality.
- The Stars: Values and direction.
- Revelation: A career is not just earning a living—it is about mission and legacy.
- The ocean teaches *how to live*, the stars reveal *why to live*.

Conclusion: Becoming a Watcher of the Ocean and the Stars
- A career is not a straight line but a vast ocean.
- You cannot control the tides, but you can choose your stance.
- The ocean makes you face reality, the stars give you meaning.
- May you finally become—

a Watcher of the Ocean and the Stars.

Chapter One: Opening Fable

I. Dawn on the Shore

Morning by the sea, the air heavy with the salt of damp mist.
The sky still held the fading traces of night, but from the east a line of gold tore across the horizon.
The sun rose slowly, and the waves rolled in, one after another, breaking upon the sand in steady rhythm—like an eternal song.

Kaito stood quietly at the edge of the shore.
His shoes were already buried in fine sand, the cuffs of his trousers dampened by spray.
Yesterday, he was still a student; today, he stood at the crossroads of life, forced to face that unfamiliar word—*career*.

"The sea is so vast..."
He whispered softly.
The ocean before him stretched without end, as boundless and uncertain as the future itself.

II. Four Figures

As he hesitated, four figures appeared along the shore.

(1) The Beach Walker
The first held a bright parasol, strolling lazily in sandals across the sand.
He smiled at Kaito and said:
"Young man, don't go into the sea. There are undercurrents, sharks, storms. It's safest here on shore. Watch the view, watch others swim—why take the risk yourself?"

His words carried the tone of comfort and complacency.
Kaito felt a heaviness in his chest. Safety, yes—but was that all there was to life?

(2) The Swimmer
Next came a woman, her skin bronzed by the sun, strong and lively.
She had just come out of the water, droplets sparkling as she laughed.

"Don't hesitate!" she called. "Jump in first. At the beginning you may only float, but as long as you keep moving, you won't sink. Life is the same—don't overthink it, just act."

Her eyes were bright with vitality and simple confidence.
Kaito's heart stirred. Perhaps she was right, yet a question lingered—was constant struggle in the waves enough to sustain a life?

(3) The Diver

The third figure bore heavy oxygen tanks, clad in a thick wetsuit, his steps steady.
He placed a hand on Kaito's shoulder and said:
"You'll never see the true world in shallow waters. In the depths lie treasures and wonders unseen by others. But beware—without preparation you'll suffocate, lose your way, perhaps even die."

Kaito's heart shook. The promise of adventure was alluring, but danger was close at hand.

(4) The Ocean Researcher

Last came a woman with glasses, holding a telescope and a sea chart. Calm, composed.
"The sea is not only for swimming or diving," she said with a gentle smile.
"It has currents, storms, and seasons. Learn to read them, and you will know where to go. Knowledge is your vessel; wisdom, your sail."

Her voice was quiet but carried a depth that seemed to echo the ocean itself.

III. Kaito's Confusion

All four spoke truth, yet none offered certainty.
Safety on the beach. Action in the shallows. Adventure in the depths. Wisdom from charts.
Which was right?

Kaito felt something pressing against his chest.
What if he chose wrongly?
What if, after years of effort, he found himself only drifting, swept by forces beyond him?

The ocean no longer seemed mere scenery, but a vast, invisible test.

IV. The Watcher

As he wavered, a white-haired old man approached slowly.
His name was **Fukuda Satoshi**, but people called him *The Watcher*.
He carried no parasol, no swim gear, no books—only a pair of clear, steady eyes.
His steps were unhurried, as if tempered by countless storms.

The old man stood beside Kaito, gazing at the horizon. His voice was low but firm:
"My child, the sea is not something to conquer, but something to understand."

Kaito froze.

"Some will spend their lives on the sand," Fukuda Satoshi continued.
"Some drift upon the waves. Some dare to dive deep. Others draw maps.
None are entirely right or wrong. But the true question is this—*Where do you wish to be? Who do you wish to become?*"

The words crashed into Kaito like a wave.
Suddenly he saw: the problem was not the answers others gave, but the life he chose for himself.

V. The Ocean's Echo

Kaito closed his eyes and listened to the waves.
They no longer roared, but whispered gently:
"Do you hear? Your path must be your own."

He opened his eyes again.
The sea shimmered, no longer a terrifying abyss but an unfinished canvas.
And the brush was in his hands.

VI. The Lesson of the Fable

This story was not only Kaito's.
Everyone who stands at life's threshold faces their own ocean.

Some choose the safety of the beach.
Some choose endless drifting.
Some choose the danger of the depths.
Some choose the wisdom of charts.

The Watcher reminds us: no one decides for you.
You must find your own place.

So it is in careers.
So it is in life.

VII. Epilogue

The wind swept over the shore. The waves rolled on, eternal.
Kaito drew a deep breath, and a faint but resolute smile rose upon his lips.

His journey had only just begun.

Chapter Two: The Beach Walker

Kaito walked on with **Fukuda Satoshi**, the Watcher.
The wind blew, erasing their footprints as quickly as they were made.

Ahead, a young man lounged in a beach chair.
He wore dark sunglasses, a heavy book resting on his lap.
Beside him lay brand-new swim shoes and a bright float board.
An umbrella shaded him from the sun. He looked comfortable, almost content.

Kaito asked curiously:
"Who is he?"

Fukuda Satoshi smiled faintly.
"His name is **Akira**. He is a Beach Walker—someone who never leaves the shore."

The Routine of Akira

Every day, Akira came to the same spot.
He brought iced water, snacks, sometimes novels or magazines.
Day after day, the pattern repeated until it became his life.

He loved watching others swim.
Some would return, laughing about being knocked over by waves.
Some would proudly show off small fish or shells.
Some spoke excitedly of underwater sights:
"A sea turtle swam right past me!"
"The waves were huge today—I almost got dragged out!"
"I dove to the bottom; there were colorful corals like another world."

Akira listened with delight. His eyes shone with longing, but his feet never moved.

"Too dangerous," he always muttered.
"I can't swim—I'd drown. Safer here on the sand."

He had even bought goggles, a life ring, a wetsuit—all piled unused in a corner, gathering dust.

The Argument for Safety

Kaito stepped closer.
"Akira, why don't you ever go in? Don't you want to experience it yourself?"

Akira lifted his sunglasses, shrugged, and replied lightly:
"Why should I? I hear the stories, don't I? Their adventures—those are enough for me.
Besides, on shore I won't be overturned by waves, won't meet sharks, won't choke on salt water. Safety first."

"But isn't that just living in imagination?" Kaito pressed.

Akira smiled.
"At least I'm secure. Isn't safety what matters most?"

Fukuda Satoshi sighed softly.
"Safety is why many remain on shore.
They fear failure. They fear being swept by waves, losing direction.
So they choose to watch, to talk, but never to act."

The Cost of Staying Ashore

Suddenly, a commotion erupted nearby.
Several swimmers returned, carrying a strange shell, shimmering with rainbow colors.

"Incredible! A treasure from the deep!"
They passed it around, marveling at its beauty.

Akira's eyes lit up with envy.
"If only I had one too…"

But he didn't rise. He looked back down at the sand, convincing himself:
"No matter. I'll just hear their stories. That's enough."

Fukuda Satoshi turned to Kaito.
"This is the cost of staying ashore.
They gain safety, but lose true opportunity.

In careers, too, there are Beach Walkers:
They envy promotions, but never learn new skills.
They complain of no opportunities, but never take the first step.
They imagine futures, but never act.
And so, they watch others sail away, while they remain behind, tide after tide."

Akira's Past

Kaito studied Akira and asked quietly:
"Have you really never tried? Not once?"

Akira hesitated, then murmured:
"When I was a child, my father took me into the water. A wave knocked me over. I swallowed water, thought I would die. Someone pulled me out, but ever since, I've never dared again."

Kaito suddenly understood.
It wasn't laziness—it was fear.
Fear that built a wall so high Akira had caged himself for life.

Fukuda Satoshi shook his head.
"The shadow of failure builds walls.
Stay inside too long, and that wall becomes a prison for life."

Kaito's Reflection

Kaito fell silent.
He remembered his own hesitation after graduation—how many times he avoided applying, how many times he retreated into comfort.
Was he, too, building his own invisible wall?

Fukuda Satoshi spoke gently:
"Standing on the beach is not wrong. Everyone begins somewhere.
But if you never leave, the sea will forever remain scenery, not your life."

Kaito gazed at the horizon.
A quiet question rose within him:
"Am I willing to spend my life on the sand?"

The Many Beach Walkers

Kaito looked around. He noticed Akira was not alone.
The beach was filled with others:
- Someone spent all day photographing surfers, never trying a board.
- Parents warned their children, "The sea is dangerous," dimming the spark in young eyes.
- Writers filled diaries with fantasies of ocean voyages, yet never touched the tide.

Fukuda Satoshi pointed at them:
"These are society's Beach Walkers.
Some are clever, some diligent, but they choose to remain ashore.
They fear failure, compare endlessly, criticize others—yet never confront their own fear.
Their careers ended before they even began."

Epilogue

The sun lowered, painting the sea red and gold.
Akira sat unmoved, flipping pages he didn't read.
His eyes flickered between the sea and his feet, like a bird trapped in its cage.

Kaito's heart churned.
He realized Fukuda Satoshi wasn't just speaking of Akira—he was warning *him*.

If I never take the first step, I too will become another Akira.

The wind blew, the waves rolled on.
Kaito inhaled deeply, clenching his fists.
The choice was still his to make.

Chapter Three: The Swimmer

Kaito walked on with **Fukuda Satoshi**, the Watcher.
The waves rolled steadily, crashing and retreating in rhythm. Not far ahead, a group of people splashed and swam, sometimes laughing, sometimes crying out in panic.

Fukuda pointed toward them and said quietly:
"Those are the swimmers. They've already entered the water."

1. The First Dive

Among them was a young woman named **Misaki**.
At first, she had been like Akira, pacing the beach in hesitation.
But one day, she clenched her teeth and leapt into the sea.

"Ahhh!"
A wave struck her face; she nearly swallowed water.
Desperately she flailed her arms and legs, until finally she learned to float.

"I can do it! I really can!"
Her eyes lit up with joy.
For the first time, she felt the sea lifting her body, holding her up.

It was like a young person's first step into the workplace:
- Perhaps just an entry-level position.
- Perhaps knowing nothing at the start.
- But at last, they begin, gaining their first true experience.

2. Carried by the Waves

At the beginning, Misaki swam each day with excitement.
She met many people at the surface; they floated together, chatted, and chased after waves.

But gradually, she realized something troubling.
She was always being carried by the current.
Sometimes she wanted to head east, but the tide pushed her west.
Sometimes she tried to stay near friends, only to be pulled away by unseen flows.

"Why can't I control where I'm going?" Misaki wondered.

From the shore, Fukuda Satoshi observed and spoke to Kaito:
"This is the state of most working people. They have entered the sea but lack direction. They drift with the currents.
— The company tells them what to do, and they obey.
— Others say to work harder, and they follow.
— Trends shift, and they chase them.
They know how to swim, but not how to navigate."

3. The Illusion of Safety

One day, the waves suddenly grew larger.
Swimmers cried out in fear:
"Help! I can't hold on much longer!"

Some clung to life rings, others were dragged back by friends—barely escaping disaster.

Misaki, too, was exhausted to the bone.
"I swim so hard every day, yet I keep circling the same place.
Is this... my future?"

A deep emptiness washed over her.

Fukuda Satoshi said softly:
"The dilemma of swimmers is this:
They have left the sand behind, but they remain at the surface.
They work hard, but always reactively.
They are busy, but see no destination.
Their safety is only on the surface—one strong wave, and the lack of foundation is revealed."

4. Misaki's Reflection

That evening, Misaki climbed onto the sand, sitting down beside Kaito.
She gazed at the deep blue of the sea, her eyes tinged with longing.

"I want to dive down, to see the world beneath," she whispered.
"But I'm afraid. The deeper you go, the greater the danger. I don't know if I can."

Kaito's heart trembled.

- Swimming allowed her to see more than those on the beach.
- But if she only floated, one day she would surely lose her way.

Fukuda Satoshi nodded.
"Most people remain swimmers for life.
They go further than those on shore, but still only skim the surface.
Only those who dare to dive deeper will touch the ocean's true secrets."

5. The Choice

Night fell, and moonlight glittered across the sea.
In her hands, Misaki held a pair of unused diving goggles, clutching them tightly.

"Maybe," she said to Kaito, "I should try diving."

Kaito gave no reply.
He simply lifted his eyes to the distant deep waters, as a question rose in his heart:

"Am I willing to remain a swimmer forever?"

Chapter Four: The Diver

The sea at dawn was vast and calm.
The horizon glowed faintly gold as waves pressed and withdrew, like the breath of some giant being. **Kaito** stood with **Fukuda Satoshi** on the shore, watching a figure step steadily into the water, burdened with heavy equipment.

"Who is he?" Kaito asked.

"That is **Kenji**," Fukuda answered with a faint smile.
"A man who chose not to remain on the surface. A Diver."

1. The First Breath Below

Kenji had once been just another swimmer, drifting on the surface, envying those who returned from the deep with stories of coral, shipwrecks, and creatures that glowed like living stars.

But one morning, he strapped on a heavy tank, secured his mask, and entered the sea.
A wave passed over him; his ears throbbed with pressure, his breath quickened.
Bubbles streamed from his mouth, rising like silver beads into the dim light.

This was the deep.

Sunlight fractured into broken shards, spilling downward. The seabed spread before him, corals like sleeping giants, fish flickering like sparks. It was a world apart from the surface.

Just like in a career, the first deep dive is when one finally leaves surface-level tasks and truly specializes:
- The first time decoding a complex financial model.
- The first time writing code that actually solves a real problem.
- The first time producing research of genuine value.

In that moment, Kenji saw a world that the swimmers could never see.

2. Beauty and Risk

The deeper he swam, the stranger and more beautiful the sights.
Coral forests swayed like cathedrals. Blue tangs darted past like painted arrows. A squid vanished behind a cloud of ink, like a curtain dropping in the middle of a play.

But danger came with it:
- **Pressure** built with depth, squeezing lungs and mind.
- **Currents** pulled suddenly, invisible ropes jerking him sideways.
- **Shadows** circled in the distance, predator or phantom, he could not tell.

For a moment, fear seized him.
"Should I ascend now, or push on?"

On the shore, Fukuda Satoshi spoke softly:
"The Diver's world is brighter and richer than the surface, but it is also more perilous.
They need stronger equipment—like real expertise, lifelong learning, independent thought.
They must master rhythm—when to descend, when to return, when to pause.
Without preparation, the pressure will crush them."

Kaito listened, his chest tightening with both awe and dread.

3. The Loneliness of Depth

In time, Kenji adapted. He could read the currents, navigate coral labyrinths, even discover hidden caverns glowing with strange light.

But when he surfaced and shared his discoveries, the responses stung him.
"Too dangerous—I'd never try that."
"Corals? Fish? Hard to imagine, really."
"Is it worth it? Easier to sip juice on the beach."

Kenji felt a heavy loneliness.
Those who had never descended could not understand what he had seen.

Fukuda Satoshi told Kaito:
"The Diver's greatest challenge is not the sea, but solitude.

Others cannot grasp what they've witnessed. They may even mock them.
Yet only Divers see truths hidden from the surface."

It is the same in work:
Specialists are called "obsessive," "too rigid."
But they are the ones who push boundaries, uncovering the hidden structures beneath.

4. The Treasure and Its Weight

One day, deep in the reefs, Kenji found an ancient pearl oyster, its shell scarred by years, holding a luminous gem within.

He did not seize it immediately.
He marked the site, checked his air, resurfaced to rest, and only later returned— careful, patient, deliberate.

When the pearl gleamed under the sun, gasps rose from swimmers and beach-walkers alike.
Some crowded to learn his methods; others stood apart, envious but silent.

Fukuda Satoshi said:
"This is the Diver's value.
They accept pressure in order to bring back true treasure.
In a career, Divers are the backbone—accumulating knowledge, creating innovation.
But the deeper you go, the more discipline you need.
Never lose yourself. Never forget to breathe."

Kaito stared at the pearl, realizing that **true value is not luck but the outcome of depth, patience, and discipline.**

5. The Pressure Test

On another dive, the sea turned cloudy, visibility vanishing.
Kenji slowed himself with three commands:
Stop—halt movement, avoid panic.
Stabilize—adjust buoyancy, steady breathing.
Judge—check depth, air, time, then decide to continue or retreat.

He chose retreat, surfacing by an alternate route.

Kaito understood something new: **retreat is part of true skill.**
Fukuda Satoshi added:
"Only those who know when to return will live to go deeper."

Kenji had passed another test. In the deep, he had learned not only to see—but to breathe.

6. Guiding Others

Soon, two swimmers asked to join him.
Kenji agreed, but he planned carefully:
- On land, he explained gear and hand signals.
- In the water, he led them in steps: five meters, eight meters, twelve meters.
- He watched their breathing more than the scenery.
- When it was time to return, he placed them ahead, himself at the rear.

He did not show them the hidden caverns yet. Instead, he gave them what they could safely handle.

Kaito, watching, understood:
A true guide is not the one who dazzles with sights, but the one who brings everyone back alive.

7. Ethics of the Deep

A merchant once begged Kenji to collect pearls for profit.
Kenji refused: "Overharvesting will destroy the reef."

The merchant persuaded others, who recklessly dove during high tide. One nearly drowned before being rescued.

Fukuda Satoshi told Kaito:
"The Diver's choice is not just what they *can* do, but what they *should* do.
Depth without ethics devours itself."

Kaito remembered the words: **Doing something right matters more than merely doing it.**

8. The Long Run

As winter came, visibility shrank.
Kenji paused his deep dives, turning to:

- Maintaining his equipment.
- Training in pools under low visibility.
- Writing careful notes of currents, depths, and risks.

Others mocked him: "Too cautious!"
He only smiled.
True depth is not one grand feat, but endurance over time.

9. Kaito's Night Question

One moonlit night, the sea was a polished blue stone.
Kaito asked softly: "I... I want to be a Diver."
"Why?" Fukuda asked.
"Because I want to see for myself—not just circle on the surface."
"And?"
"Because I don't want my fate to be decided by currents and tides."
"Still not enough." Fukuda shook his head.
"To dive, you must be ready for preparation, review, restraint, and boundaries."

Kaito fell silent for a long time. Finally, he nodded.
"I am willing."

10. The Second Pearl

On the last good day before winter, Kenji led two companions.
They did not chase treasure. Instead, they found a young sea turtle tangled in fishing line.
Kenji cut it free, tended the wound, and watched it swim slowly toward calmer waters.

When they surfaced, Kaito whispered:

"Today's greatest treasure wasn't scenery or pearls. It was knowing that in the deep, we could still choose what was right."

Kenji smiled.
"That is another kind of pearl."

Conclusion

The tide lapped at Kaito's feet. The sea was dark blue glass under the moon.

He lifted his head to the horizon. The waves gave no answer, the wind no answer.
But his heart answered for him:

*"I will learn to dive.
To prepare, to endure pressure, to know restraint, to guard boundaries.
To see truth in the deep—and return with value."*

His hands clenched, as if holding an invisible pen.
In the silence of the night sea, Kaito knew:
His journey had only just begun.

Chapter Five: The Ocean Researcher

I. A Visitor at Sea

The morning tide hummed like a slow, growing song, spilling over the shore and drawing back, leaving foam and shells polished smooth. Kaito walked beside **Fukuda Satoshi**, his footprints already swallowed by the retreating surf.

He had not slept much. The image of **Kenji the Diver**, wrestling with undercurrents in the deep, still replayed in his mind. That choice—whether to risk or retreat—felt like a pearl lodged in his chest, glowing faintly and refusing to vanish.

Fukuda suddenly stopped.
"Look out there."

Across the glimmering surface drifted a modest research vessel, painted a quiet gray-blue. At its stern floated several orange buoys. On deck stood a figure: one hand steadying a telescope, the other scribbling across thick sea charts. Instruments bristled along the railings—anemometers, sampling bottles, lines dragging sensors below.

The figure raised her head. Even from shore, she seemed to recognize Fukuda. She waved, calling across the water, her voice carried clear by the wind:
"**Come aboard!** From the beach, you'll never hear the ocean's heartbeat."

Fukuda smiled, eyes soft with recognition.
"She is **Suwaka**. An old friend. Let's pay her a visit."

Moments later, a dinghy ferried them across. Climbing the ladder, Kaito was immediately struck by the vessel's orderliness:
- Charts weighted down under transparent covers.
- Notebooks crammed with notes: *wind speed, tide height, current velocity, sea surface temperature.*
- An acoustic Doppler profiler humming near the bow.
- A radar mast turning lazily above.

"**Satoshi.**" The woman set down her pen, stepping forward with a smile. "After all these years, I'd know your footsteps through any gale."

"Suwaka." Fukuda clasped her hand. His weathered skin pressed against hers. "And you still spread your charts like you're preparing for battle."

"With the sea," she replied warmly, "every day is a war without smoke."

Then her eyes turned to Kaito.
"So you are the one he calls *Kaido*. Welcome aboard. Don't just watch from the sand. Stand here, and you'll feel the sea breathe."

II. The Old Friends

"You two… know each other from long ago?" Kaito asked.

"Long enough," Suwaka said with a half-smile, "that we've fought more times than I can count."

"In our youth," she continued, "I dived endlessly, convinced that every answer lay in one more coral cave, one more trench. And he—" she pointed at Fukuda—"he told me: *The deeper you go, the smaller the world becomes.* I hated hearing that. I thought he was belittling my courage."

Fukuda chuckled, eyes glinting. "Until the storm."

Suwaka nodded. "Yes, the storm. The sea lay flat as a mirror that morning. I saw signs—cloud banks forming too fast, a strange chill in the breeze. I told him a squall was coming. He laughed at my 'paranoia.' Two hours later, the sky collapsed. A wall of wind. A returning wave. We would have lost lives if we hadn't moved people to the lee of the rip current's outlet. That day, I learned to read from the deck. He learned that watching can save as much as warning."

Kaito looked at them with new respect. Friendship, he realized, wasn't about never clashing. It was about *witnessing each other become what they needed most.*

III. Lessons on Deck

Suwaka led Kaito to the bow. She pointed to the Doppler profiler's screen.
"See this? Not one current, but layers stacked like sheets. Surface water eastward, bottom water westward, the middle oscillating with wind shear. If you only swim,

you'll think you're fighting the tide. But what you're really fighting is the mismatch between layers."

She placed his eye to a handheld anemometer.
"Wind, south by east. That means today or tomorrow, a coastal current will form, pushing debris north. A swimmer will swear he's trying his best, but still he'll drift away. That's not weakness. That's physics."

She spread a year-long chart before him. Arrows, circles, arcs, scribbled numbers. "These aren't decorations. These lines are tidal amplitudes. These arrows, dominant flows. These shaded lobes—eddies, always forming in the same coves. If you only dive, you'll touch wonder. If you only swim, you'll taste salt. But if you read—really read—you'll see a system."

"What's the most important ability for a researcher?" Kaito asked.

Suwaka tilted her head. "What's the most important ability for a diver?"

"Breath. Process. Retreat," he answered quickly.

"Exactly. Researchers too:
- **Breath**: Don't drown in data. Pause. Let judgment breathe.
- **Process**: Sampling, calibration, cross-checking. Skip one step, and you have a beautiful lie.
- **Retreat**: When data contradicts belief, retreat. Start again."

She paused. "And add two more: **questions** and **names.** Ask the right question, and you'll gather the right samples. Name a phenomenon, and you give others a way to share it. Fear ends the moment we can speak its name."

Fukuda nodded quietly. "Reproducibility. That's the honesty of research."

IV. Storm Before Sunset

By afternoon, winds shifted faster than expected. The profiler showed rising bottom currents. Suwaka's brows furrowed.
"Half an hour earlier than I thought," she muttered.

Orders came swiftly:

"Check buoy one. Stable. Buoy two—weak signal. Satoshi, alert the lifeguard station. Hoist the yellow flag. Kaito, help me deploy a cross-shore line. We need another profile."

Across the bay, several small boats gathered, preparing for a night paddle they called *The Moonlight Row*. Laughter carried over the waves.

Suwaka seized a loudhailer:
"Pull back! Tonight, a rip current will form in the bay mouth!"

The rowers waved dismissively, unconcerned.

"They won't believe us," Kaito said anxiously.

"They don't need to believe me," Suwaka replied. "They need to see proof."

Minutes later, buoy one's red light began to flash rapidly. A boat suddenly lurched outward, sucked by an invisible ribbon of water. Paddlers screamed, oars flailing.

"Steer sideways! Cross, not back!" Suwaka shouted, positioning her vessel at the rip's edge to open a channel. Fukuda relayed coordinates ashore. Kaito watched, breath held, as the small craft slipped out of the rip and into safety.

On deck, Suwaka turned to the rescued group, voice low but firm:
"You can doubt a person. But you cannot doubt **data**."

For the first time, Kaito saw knowledge turn into a backbone of action— observation, warning, rescue, education—seamlessly linked within minutes.

V. Knowledge and Temptation

Not long after, a businessman boarded the vessel, eyeing Suwaka's maps.
"These are exquisite. My company will pay handsomely for a route. We want the prime migration corridor of ribbonfish. Just one line from you, and our ships will be full for three seasons."

"And the flanking zones?" Suwaka asked coolly.

The man hesitated. "They... house juveniles. But we only catch the adults."

"No. That line is a knife. And knives are neutral, but people are not. If I hand you this, you will gut the nursery as surely as the corridor."

"We'll donate, sponsor, build schools—"

"Donations to ease guilt are not the purpose of science." Suwaka rolled up the chart. "I refuse."

The man left scowling.

Kaito said nothing. But inside, he saw clearly: **knowledge is power, but responsibility is its weight.**

Fukuda placed a hand on his shoulder. "Remember: between *can* and *should* lies humanity; between *know* and *guard* lies conscience."

VI. The Honest Word: "Uncertain"

That night, under the dim cabin light, Suwaka transcribed the day's numbers—wind, tide, salinity, anomalies, outcomes, future notes. Page after page, like rivets bolting today to tomorrow.

Kaito asked quietly, "You do this every day?"

"Every single day. Not for papers, not for fame. For **replication.** If someone else cannot repeat my steps, then I have left them a story, not science."

He hesitated. "And the parts you don't understand?"

Suwaka pointed at a blank corner of the chart. "Here. Every autumn turning to winter, stratification strengthens suddenly. I don't know why. Maybe cold fronts. Maybe internal tides. I'm not sure."

Kaito expected her to cover uncertainty. Instead, she said it plainly.

"Uncertainty is the researcher's most honest posture. Admit it, and you'll keep asking. Pretend certainty, and you'll build danger."

VII. Naming Fear

The next morning, Suwaka recounted an old tale.

"Years ago, outside this bay, there was a 'curse.' Every season, boats vanished in the same strip. People whispered myths. I almost believed them.

"But Satoshi and I spent three months running thirty-six surveys. It wasn't a curse. It was topography and monsoon, creating a standing current. We mapped it. Marked it with two red flags. And from that year forward, no one called it a curse. They called it **Red Flag.**"

Fukuda added softly: "To name is to drag fear out of the dark. A name gives people a way to mention it, and a way to warn each other."

Kaito realized: researchers don't just put the sea on paper. They put the sea into people's **choices.**

VIII. Carrying the Chart Ashore

On the third day, Suwaka rolled up a carefully drawn *Rip Current Warning Map* and pressed it into Kaito's arms.
"Take this ashore. Pin it on the lifeguard board. Let it belong to everyone."

Kaito held it like a living thing. He remembered his old charts—project timelines, KPI spreadsheets, financial ledgers. Those had been tools to **control people**. This one was to **protect them.**

Suwaka said, "There are two kinds of charts: ones researchers make for themselves, and ones they make for **non-researchers**. The latter is harder. You must translate complexity into action. Fail at that, and your research never existed."

Kaito nodded solemnly.

IX. From Me to Us

That evening, Suwaka handed Kaito a blank logbook.
"From today, you are no longer a guest. You are our **record keeper.** Sign your name."

Kaito signed. His chest tightened as though he'd tied his life to the sea itself.

"What does it mean?" he asked.

"It means your name now belongs to this coast. These logs will be given to schools, lifeguards, whoever wants them. Every line you write adds to their safety. From now on, you don't study only for yourself."

Kaito pressed the book to his chest like a stone that radiated warmth.

X. The Ocean Between Friends

As dusk fell, Fukuda and Suwaka stood at the stern, watching Kaito arrange equipment for tomorrow. For a while they said nothing, listening to the engine tick down.

Suwaka finally spoke. "Thank you for bringing him. His eyes are open, but so is his heart. Rarely do both stay awake together."

"And thank you," Fukuda replied, "for giving him a map. I can show him how to look. You can show him how to see."

She chuckled. "You still turn simple things into proverbs."

"Then let me give you another: alone, I guard; with you, I guide."

They laughed quietly, their old quarrels softened by the years. The Watcher and the Researcher—no longer roles opposed, but shoulders joined.

XI. Epilogue: From Understanding to Navigation

The next dawn, the vessel dropped anchor near shore. Suwaka pressed the map tube firmly into Kaito's hands.
"Take it. Tell them this: winds will shift, currents will turn, but if we are willing to learn, the ocean always offers windows of safe passage."

"I will," Kaito promised. "I'll pin it, and I'll tell every swimmer what it means."

"Don't forget to tell them your own story," Fukuda added. "People believe more when they see another person take the first step. Only then will they listen to the second."

As they disembarked, the horizon glowed with lingering red, the sea kissing the sky without seam.

Kaito looked back at the small research vessel. Not a grand ship, but it glowed like a steadfast lighthouse. He realized at last: **the Beach Walker, the Swimmer, the Diver, the Researcher—none were enemies. They were all positions on the same map.**

Some took the first step. Some ventured deeper. Some brought treasures back. Some linked the dots into a whole, turning personal safety into collective safety.

He hugged the map tube close, the wind cool and salted against his cheek.

I am not here to conquer the ocean, he thought. *I am here to walk with it.*

And so, the journey continued.

Chapter Six: The Practitioner · The Watcher

1. Night on the Shore

Night slowly fell upon the sea.
The last glow of the sun had sunk beneath the horizon, leaving a sky strewn with stars reflected in the waves. Kaito sat beside Fukuda Satoshi on a large rock by the shore, listening to the rhythm of waves striking against stone. The salty air filled his lungs, sharp and cleansing.

Far out on the horizon, Suwaka's research vessel carried a small, steady light, drifting like a firefly in the dark. It reminded Kaito that some people still ventured outward to study and map the ocean, while the man beside him had chosen to remain on land.

At last, Kaito spoke, unable to hold back the question in his chest.
"Fukuda-san, why do you remain here watching the sea? You are not like Akira, content to sit on the beach. You no longer swim like Misaki, struggling with the waves. You do not dive like Kenji, carrying heavy equipment into the depths. You don't even chart the ocean like Suwaka. You just... sit here and watch. What meaning is there in that?"

Fukuda Satoshi smiled gently, his gaze calm, steady as stone weathered by tides.
"Child, I have done all those things. I swam, I dove, I studied. But in the end, I returned to the shore—not because I gave up, but because someone must remain here. Someone must hold the light."

2. The Meaning of Watching

Fukuda picked up an old oil lamp resting beside him.
He struck a match, touched it to the wick, and a flame bloomed. The wind made it sway, but it did not go out. Raising the lamp high toward the sea, he spoke:

"When someone loses their way at night, this light gives them direction.
When storms rise, it becomes a warning.
When the young step into the waves for the first time, it shows them how not to be crushed by the surf.

Watching is not withdrawal—it is to **become a lighthouse for others.**"

Kaito's eyes widened.
"A lighthouse…"

Fukuda nodded.
"In the world of careers, a Watcher is a Practitioner—one who has lived, one who has learned, and one who now gives back.
They have experience and they have insight.
They know how to stand alone, but they also know how to steady others.
They see not only the sea's waves, but the hearts of those who venture into them."

3. The Power of the Lamp

At that moment, a child came running along the beach, breathless, crying.
"Grandfather! My brother—he's been swept away by the waves!"

Without hesitation, Fukuda lifted the oil lamp high, swinging it back and forth.
The trembling flame cut through the dark, a signal against the backdrop of stars.

Far out in the water, a struggling swimmer caught sight of the light. Gasping, he shifted course, forcing his tired arms to follow its glow. At last, he staggered ashore, collapsing into the sand.

The younger brother flung himself at him, sobbing. The swimmer, pale but alive, bowed deeply.
"If not for that light, I would not have found my way back."

Kaito felt his heart shiver.
For the first time, he understood: **a Watcher is not idle. A Watcher saves lives— with knowledge, with wisdom, with a lamp held steady against the dark.**

4. The Path to Becoming a Watcher

Kaito turned to him, voice hushed but earnest.
"Fukuda-san… how can I become like you? How can I be a Watcher?"

Fukuda gazed at the lamp.
"To be a Watcher, you must walk three stages of the sea.

1.   **Learn to swim.** Step into the ocean. Know reality. Feel the waves against your body.
2.   **Learn to dive.** Enter the depths. Study deeply. Endure pressure and loneliness.
3.   **Learn to research.** Raise your head. See the whole, understand currents and storms.

And then—return to the shore. Lift a lamp.
That is the Watcher's role. Not for themselves, but for others."

Each word fell like a stone into Kaito's chest, sending ripples through his heart.

5. Watchers in Every Field

Fukuda's voice grew slower, firmer.
"In every industry there are Watchers.
They are the mentors who guide the young.
They are the elders who share their lessons.
They are the guardians who protect a healthy course for the group.
  •   They do not seek the spotlight, but they help others go further.
  •   They do not cling to their own glory, but they guard the path of the many.
  •   They know the sea is not meant to be conquered alone—it is meant to be crossed together.

The truest value is not in conquering the ocean for oneself, but in ensuring many others may sail it safely."

Kaito's mind filled with images:
  •   Akira, stuck forever on the beach, only envying others.
  •   Misaki, tossed and turned by waves, always swimming but never steering.
  •   Kenji, venturing into the depths, heavy with equipment, lonely in pressure.
  •   Suwaka, aboard her vessel, mapping the whole, pointing to safe routes.

And now Fukuda—the one who chose to remain, lamp in hand, guarding the rest.

6. Fukuda's Story

After a pause, Kaito asked softly:
"Fukuda-san... were you once like them too?"

Fukuda's eyes wandered toward the dark horizon. His voice carried the weight of memory.
"Yes. When I was young, I thought speed mattered most. I swam against others, eager to prove myself. Later, I carried tanks and plunged into the depths, amazed at sights no one else had seen. After that, I boarded ships like Suwaka's, drawing maps, believing I had finally mastered the ocean.

But the sea is endless. No matter how far I swam, how deep I dove, how precise my maps—there was always more. And worse, I saw many perish because of ignorance, arrogance, or blind ambition.

That was when I understood: my mission was not to conquer the sea, but to guard those who came after. To stand here, and hold a light."

Kaito sat still, listening, his respect deepening with every word.

7. Kaito's Awakening

The wind blew. The flame wavered but did not die.

Kaito stared at it, a longing rising within.
"Fukuda-san... one day, I want to be like you. I want to be a Watcher."

Fukuda nodded slowly, his eyes as deep as the sea.
"Then begin now.
Find your place in the ocean.
Learn to endure the waves.
And when the time comes, hold up your lamp.

That lamp will light the path for others—
and it will light your own as well."

8. Conclusion

In Kaito's mind, five figures stood clear:

- **Akira, the Beach Walker**: forever on the sand, envying but never moving.
- **Misaki, the Swimmer**: brave but aimless, pushed wherever the waves take her.
- **Kenji, the Diver**: deep in skill, enduring pressure and solitude.
- **Suwaka, the Researcher**: charting the sea, seeing patterns, drawing maps.
- **Fukuda Satoshi, the Watcher**: back on shore, lamp in hand, guiding all.

Fukuda's final words echoed like the surf:
"The sea's meaning is not conquest, but understanding.
The value of watching is not in personal glory, but in the safety of the many.
Remember, child: life and career are oceans.
The strongest are not those who go farthest alone—
but those who help many travel farther together."

Kaito lifted his head. Stars glimmered above.
In that moment, he felt them merge with the flame of Fukuda's lamp, weaving together into a single radiance—
a light to guide the voyage ahead.

Chapter Seven: Up, Down, Left, Right — Your Coordinates in the Industry

1. A Question Beneath the Stars

The night grew deep.
The tide whispered against the rocks, and the sky spilled its stars onto the rolling sea. Kaito sat beside Fukuda Satoshi on a weathered boulder. The salt wind stung his lips, and far off, the faint lamp on Suwaka's vessel blinked like a patient eye.

At last Kaito asked, his voice hushed but urgent:
"Fukuda-san, you've told me about the Beach Walker, the Swimmer, the Diver, the Researcher, and the Watcher. But in such a vast ocean, how do I know where I truly stand? How can I be sure I'm moving in the right direction?"

Fukuda gazed out at the horizon. His silence was long, like the pause before a wave breaks. Then he smiled faintly.
"Kaito, at sea the greatest danger is not the waves, but losing your sense of direction. You must always know your **up, down, left, and right**. Only then can you find your coordinates."

2. Upward: The Sky and Vision

Fukuda raised his hand toward the stars. The Big Dipper gleamed above, ancient and unshaken.
"In the age of sail, navigators guided themselves by the stars. Without the sky, ships drifted aimlessly."

He turned to Kaito.
"In careers, the sky is your vision, your long-term goal."

Kaito thought of Misaki. She had leapt boldly into the water, brimming with enthusiasm, but soon she was tossed about by waves, following currents she could not control. She never once looked up to the stars.

"Many people live busy lives yet have no direction.
They stare only at the foam before them—today's salary, tomorrow's title—and forget to ask what they truly want to become.

But those who lift their eyes to the sky, even if progress is slow, never lose their way."

Fukuda's gaze pierced the dark.
"So I ask you, Kaito: what is your sky? Do you wish to be an expert? An entrepreneur? A researcher? Or, one day, a Watcher?"

3. Downward: The Seabed and Foundations

Fukuda picked up a smooth stone from the sand, worn round by countless tides. "This stone was shaped by years at the bottom. The seabed is foundation."

He paused.
"In a career, the seabed is your skills, your values, your integrity. Without it, any ambition above will collapse."

He told Kaito about Kenji.
Kenji once plunged recklessly, swept by currents, nearly suffocated. Only after years of training and equipping himself did he truly become a Diver, able to return with treasures from the deep.

"Many people chase upward, striving for higher titles and loftier goals, but forget to sink downward and anchor themselves. Without roots, they are like seaweed— swept away at the first surge."

Fukuda's eyes lingered on Kaito.
"Where is your foundation? Are you building it every day? If you dream of becoming a Watcher, you must first learn to plant your roots."

4. Leftward: Companions and Partners

From afar, laughter drifted over the waves. A group of young swimmers were moving together, their splashes echoing in unison.

Fukuda nodded toward them.
"Left is for companions. The ocean is vast; swim alone, and exhaustion will eventually claim you. But with companions, you can cross farther waters."

He explained:

"In careers, colleagues are partners, mentors are guides, even rivals can be forces that push you forward. True professionals know how to remain independent while drawing strength from others."

Kaito remembered Suwaka.
Her maps were not born of solitary study alone but of years working with a team of observers, sailors, and scholars. Without them, her sea charts could never have been complete.

Fukuda's tone softened.
"Who are your companions? Are you walking alone, or have you found your team? Remember, a Watcher's lamp only matters if there are people willing to see its light."

5. Rightward: The Unknown and Opportunity

The wind shifted, carrying a strange scent. Kaito looked out and saw the sea glimmer with a pale light in the far distance, as if hiding an unseen island.

Fukuda smiled knowingly.
"Right is for the unknown, for opportunities yet untried. It is where danger and discovery live side by side."

He spoke of Akira.
Akira had lived his whole life on the sand, watching others return with treasures, but never dared step into the unknown. And so, his life was filled with envy but empty of discovery.

"Many people fear the unknown, so they stop moving. Others dare to venture, and they find new islands, unseen corals, and hidden pearls. In careers, the unknown is new industries, new skills, new roles."

His voice grew firm.
"Do you leave yourself the courage to explore to the right? If not, you will circle the same waters forever."

6. The Wisdom of Coordinates

Fukuda bent down and drew a large cross in the sand, a compass of sorts. He tapped each direction with his finger.

"A person who looks only one way will be lost:
— Only the sky, and they forget their foundation.
— Only the seabed, and they miss the horizon.
— Only companions, and they lose independence.
— Only the unknown, and they forfeit stability.

The wisdom of a career is to see all four—up, down, left, right—and to know your coordinates."

Kaito stared at the cross traced in the sand. Something within him loosened, as if fog had lifted.

7. Drawing Your Career Map

Fukuda handed Kaito a sheet of paper.
"Now, draw your coordinates. Make your own map."

Kaito obeyed, his hand trembling slightly.
- At the center, he wrote his name: **Kaito**.
- Above, he wrote his vision: *to one day become a Watcher who lights the way for others.*
- Below, he listed his roots: *writing, research, honesty, patience.*
- To the left, he wrote the names of companions: *Suwaka, Kenji, Misaki, and others who journey beside me.*
- To the right, he left a space blank, writing only: *the unknown I have yet to dare.*

When he finished, he felt something he had not felt in months—stability.
His life was no longer a drift in boundless water. He had coordinates, a chart, a compass.

8. Epilogue: Finding His Place

The stars gleamed brighter, as though approving his map. Fukuda gently lowered the lamp, its flame steady against the wind.

"Remember this, Kaito.

Careers are not straight lines—they are seas.
When you see your up, down, left, and right, you will not be swept adrift. You will know where you are.

And when you know where you are—
you can go farther than you ever dreamed."

Kaito raised his head. The horizon stretched wide, the sea unending, but for the first time, he felt no fear.
He had a map, a lamp beside him, and the stars above.
He had found his coordinates.

Chapter Eight: Currents and Undercurrents — The Power of Environment

Prologue: A Lesson from Night Sailing

Night draped its veil over the sea.
The sky was heavy and deep, stars scattered across it like ancient lanterns. The ocean rolled with a rhythm of its own, each wave sounding like a low drumbeat in an eternal symphony.

Kaito stood on the deck, gripping the cold railing until his knuckles turned white. The wind carried the salty, metallic scent of the ocean straight into his lungs. His heart was caught between reverence and unease.

Beside him stood **Fukuda Satoshi**—his hair white, his eyes calm yet piercing. He wore an old navy coat, its hem flapping like a banner in the wind. His presence was steady, like a mountain that had stood against countless storms.

Kaito broke the silence.
"Sensei, I always thought sailing depended on us—on our arms, our sails, our willpower. But tonight, I noticed the ship sometimes speeds up without effort, and sometimes it struggles no matter how hard we row. Why?"

Fukuda gazed at the dark sea as though listening to its whispers. After a long pause, he spoke, his voice low and resolute:

"Child, remember this: at sea, what decides your direction and speed is not your arms, but the **currents and undercurrents**. Invisible, yet stronger than any man's effort."

The words struck Kaito like a wave. For the first time, he understood: effort mattered, but the unseen forces of the environment—the tides, the flows—shaped destiny far more profoundly.

Section 1: Surface Currents — The Push of Trends

The research vessel slid into a warm current. Suddenly the ship surged forward with little need for adjustment, carried effortlessly.

Young crew members cheered. "Our steering is perfect tonight!"

Fukuda shook his head, smiling faintly. "It isn't your brilliance—it's the current pushing you. You are only borrowing its strength."

Kaito peered over the side. The water shimmered slightly warmer, faster, its ripples urgent beneath the moonlight. A realization dawned: surface currents were the visible trends of the sea.

Fukuda pointed outward.
"In life and career, surface currents are like **policy, markets, and technology**.
— When a nation backs renewable energy, whole industries surge overnight.
— When consumer habits shift online, e-commerce explodes.
— When breakthroughs in AI or biotech arrive, new professions bloom while old ones vanish.

These forces are not for you to resist or command. They decide where your journey is easier—or harder."

Images filled Kaito's mind:
- Textile industries fleeing the West for Asia, feeding millions of families.
- The internet's rise, when youths with one computer overturned entire industries.
- Today's AI revolution, erasing some roles while birthing others.

He whispered, half to himself, "If I don't see the current... does that mean I'll be swimming against it?"

Fukuda nodded. "Exactly. Many toil for years, yet feel stuck. It is not laziness—it is because they never realized they were caught in the wrong current."

Section 2: Undercurrents — The Hidden Forces

The next morning, the sea looked calm as glass. Encouraged, Kaito dove in to train. The sun was bright, the water clear.

At first, he swam smoothly. Then, without warning, a force tugged at his legs. Invisible yet relentless, it dragged him sideways. The harder he fought, the more exhausted he became. By the time he surfaced, gasping, he was far off course.

Fukuda, watching from the deck, sighed. "That is the undertow. Silent, unseen, but powerful enough to drown the careless."

Still breathless, Kaito asked, "What are undercurrents in a career?"

Fukuda clasped his hands behind his back.
"They are the **hidden powers**:
— Organizational culture: not the written rules, but the unspoken ones that decide who rises and who leaves.
— Relationships: unseen alliances that crown some overnight while suffocating others.
— Value conflicts: when your environment contradicts your principles, draining passion until you lose yourself."

Memories struck Kaito. In internships he had seen it—hardworking colleagues ignored while others, favored by networks, advanced. Teams where support bred growth, and others where coldness bred decay.

"That," Fukuda said softly, "is the undertow. Unseen, but decisive. The wise don't fight blindly. They sense, adjust, and flow."

Section 3: Storms and Surprises — The Uncontrollable Shocks

By evening, dark clouds gathered. The sky split with lightning; waves towered like walls. The ship lurched violently as crewmen screamed.

Fukuda's voice cut through the chaos, steady and commanding:
"Reef the sails! Drop anchor! Light the signal lamp!"

Obeying, the crew steadied the vessel. They rode out the storm battered but intact, water pooling on the deck like scars of survival.

Kaito clung to the rail, trembling. "This storm… it's like disaster itself."

Fukuda nodded. "Yes. Storms are the **unexpected crises** of life and work:
— Economic crashes that cripple industries overnight.
— Companies collapsing, leaving loyal employees stranded.
— Pandemics, wars, financial shocks reshaping fate."

"You cannot stop storms. But you can prepare:
— Keep **buoyancy**: transferable skills that stop you from sinking.
— Keep a **lifeboat**: backup plans, savings, networks.
— Keep sight of the **lighthouse**: values and direction that guide you in the dark."

Section 4: The Dialogue Between Self and Environment

When calm returned, Kaito stood long at the bow, staring at the washed-clean deck.

Once he had believed, "Hard work guarantees success." But now he had seen: some reached islands effortlessly with a current, others drowned in undercurrents, and storms humbled all.

He whispered, "So effort matters, but environment decides more than I knew."

Fukuda laid a hand on his shoulder. His gaze was both stern and kind.
"Child, wisdom is not denying environment, but recognizing and using it. Only when you dance with the sea can you travel far."

Section 5: How to Dance with the Currents

Fukuda raised his hand, counting slowly:
1.   **Recognize** — See the trend. Don't pretend it isn't there.
2.   **Choose** — Ride the current to accelerate; in reverse currents, seek refuge.
3.   **Adjust** — Stay alert to undercurrents; stay calm in storms.
4.   **Guide** — When experienced, warn others: 'There lies an undertow. There, a current you can ride.'

Kaito gazed at the vast water, and for the first time he felt its invisible movements. True mastery was not brute force, but sensitivity and foresight.

Section 6: A Double Lesson

As stars reappeared, Fukuda lit a small oil lamp on the deck. Its glow flickered across the young crew's faces.

"I leave you three lessons," he said.
— To the young: Courage is not enough—cultivate sensitivity.
— To the mid-career: Effort is not enough—learn the trends.
— To the elders: Self is not enough—protect the community."

Kaito listened in silence, his chest surging with waves. He realized he was no longer merely a swimmer—he was learning to read the sea.

Epilogue: Kaito's Awakening

The night deepened. Alone on deck, Kaito let the wind lash his face. He whispered to the endless horizon:

"I don't want to rely only on muscle. I want to understand the sea."

Fukuda's silhouette appeared beside him, calm as always. He smiled faintly. "Child, when you learn to read currents and undercurrents, only then do you truly begin as a helmsman."

Kaito's heart steadied. For the first time, courage and clarity rose together within him. His voyage was no longer blind drifting—it was awakening.

Chapter Nine: Creatures of the Ocean
The Humanity and Roles Around You

I. Prologue: The Ocean Is Not Empty

The night was vast, silver starlight scattered down, and the sea shimmered like liquid glass. Haito stood on the deck, beside the Watcher Fukuda Satoshi, quietly listening to the rhythmic beat of waves striking the hull.

"I used to think the ocean only had waves, surface currents, and undercurrents," Haito admitted in a low voice.
"But the farther we sail, the clearer I see—it is alive. Everywhere there are creatures, even shaping the ocean itself."

Fukuda Satoshi smiled faintly, his voice deep and calm:
"You're right. The ocean is not a void; it is a vast ecosystem. Each creature represents a way of existence, a role. A career is the same. You are never truly alone. The people around you are like creatures in the sea: some gentle, some cruel; some huge yet harmless, some beautiful outside yet filled with poison. If you can learn to recognize them, you will find the way to survive."

II. Small Fish — Workplace Newcomers

At dawn, the ship neared shallow waters. Haito looked down and saw schools of silver fish glinting in the sunlight. They clung tightly together, swaying with the current. Once one strayed from the group, gulls would dive or bigger fish would immediately strike.

Fukuda Satoshi pointed and said:
"Those are the newcomers of the sea. In the workplace, they are the beginners.

—They imitate and learn, because they know nothing else;
—They rely on the group to survive, lacking independence;
—They are fragile, easily preyed upon, yet grow the fastest.

There is no shame in being a small fish. Everyone starts there. But if you forever rely on the school, never learning independence, you will be trapped. One day you'll realize you missed the vaster ocean."

Haito recalled his early days—nervous, clumsy, dependent on others for everything. He finally understood: being a small fish is necessary, but staying there forever is fatal.

III. Sharks — Predators

By noon, the ship sailed into deeper waters. Suddenly, a massive shadow cleaved the waves—a shark leapt from the sea, opening its cold jaws, scattering the fish. Haito instinctively stepped back.

"Sharks are predators," Fukuda Satoshi said gravely.
"They are swift, sharp, and merciless.

In the workplace, sharks are those who survive by competition and predation.
—They immediately sense others' weaknesses;
—They always strike at the critical moment, seizing opportunities;
—They win respect with strength, never with pity.

Facing sharks, remember:
—Don't expose your weaknesses casually;
—Don't expect them to protect you—they are rivals, not guardians;
—You may cooperate, even borrow their strength, but never forget their nature—sharks don't put away their teeth just because you are kind."

Haito's heart sank. He realized he had already met "sharks" in life—those who smiled outwardly but struck at crucial moments.

IV. Whales — Giants

That night, the ship suddenly shuddered. Haito peered overboard and saw a massive shadow gliding slowly beneath the vessel—a whale, as large as an island. Its steady movement shifted the rhythm of the surrounding waters, and schools of fish followed its path.

"Whales are not predators," Fukuda Satoshi said gently.
"They are huge but gentle. By sheer size alone, they alter the sea's rhythm.

In the workplace, whales symbolize industry giants or corporate leaders.
—Their vastness brings security and stability;
—Their decisions ripple through the whole ecosystem;
—Under their shelter, small fish may be protected, but also risk losing freedom.

Be careful. Life near whales may feel safe, but one day you may find yourself crushed by their weight, your space to grow taken away."

Haito nodded, recalling friends in large corporations: abundant resources and protection, yet their creativity and courage slowly faded within endless layers of hierarchy.

V. Sea Turtles — Long-Distance Runners

At dawn the next day, the sea was calm. In the distance, a sea turtle swam slowly but steadily. Its movements were unhurried, yet carried a clear sense of direction, able to cross vast oceans.

With respect, Fukuda Satoshi said:
"The sea turtle symbolizes endurance and longevity.

In the workplace, they are those who keep going for decades.
—They are never hasty, yet never stop;
—They withstand storms without losing direction;
—In the end, they reach places others never could.

If you choose to be a sea turtle, you may not be the fastest, but you are likely the one who travels the farthest."

Haito thought of scholars, craftsmen, and silent workers. They may never shine brightly, but leave the deepest marks in the river of time.

VI. Coral Reefs — Groups and Culture

By midday, the ship anchored near coral reefs. Through the clear water, Haito saw brilliant corals teeming with life. Small fish darted among the branches, shrimp busied themselves cleaning, and crabs hid in crevices, forming a bustling underwater city.

With solemnity, Fukuda Satoshi said:
"Coral itself is unremarkable, but it is the foundation of the entire ecosystem.

In the workplace, coral reefs symbolize teams and organizational culture.
—A healthy reef nurtures life and allows newcomers to grow;
—A diseased reef suffocates individuals and eventually decays;
—The reef is not one being, but an ecosystem built collectively.

Never underestimate the power of environment. A team's culture often determines fate faster than personal ability."

Haito took a deep breath. He realized that sometimes failure is not due to personal weakness, but because he was in a "poisoned reef."

VII. Poisonous Fish and Impostors

Haito was drawn to a dazzlingly bright fish. Its scales glittered like jewels, mesmerizing him. He unconsciously reached out.

"Stop!" Fukuda Satoshi pulled him back. "That's a poisonous fish. Its beauty is only a disguise—inside it hides venom."

Haito's eyes widened.

Fukuda Satoshi continued:
"In the workplace, impostors are just like that.
—Outwardly friendly, but secretly harmful;
—Saying one thing, doing another;
—At the most crucial moment, they will betray you.

Don't be deceived by appearances. True companions stand with you in storms, not push you from behind."

Haito trembled, recalling times when he trusted too quickly and tasted the bitterness of betrayal.

VIII. Haito's Realization

At night, the wind calmed. Haito leaned against the railing, silent for a long time. At last, he whispered:
"The ocean is not empty water. It is full of creatures, each with a role. So is life. The outcome depends not only on my effort, but also on how I see and choose the people around me."

Fukuda Satoshi nodded, his gaze as vast as the endless horizon:
"Exactly. You will meet small fish, sharks, whales, sea turtles, coral reefs, and impostors. Learn to tell them apart, learn to coexist. Only then can you move safely and firmly through the ocean."

IX. Summary
- Small fish: newcomers, reliant on groups.
- Sharks: predators, powerful but dangerous.
- Whales: giants, provide shelter but stifle growth.
- Sea turtles: long-distance runners, winning by endurance.
- Coral reefs: team culture, determining rise or fall.
- Impostors: double-faced, hidden risks.

A career is not an isolated island, but an ecosystem. To thrive, you must learn to coexist with different roles and find your own place within it.

Chapter Ten: Storms and Surprises
How to Face Unpredictable Career Crises

I. The Coming of the Storm

That day, the sea suddenly darkened.
The once-clear blue sky was instantly smothered by heavy clouds, as if a vast curtain had sealed the world.
Winds howled and battered the sails.
Lightning split the darkness; thunder rumbled, shaking the surface of the sea.

Waves rose as tall as houses, forming walls of water that threatened to swallow everything.

Swimmers scattered in panic, screaming.
Divers rushed to the surface, fumbling with their gear.
Researchers' charts blurred as rain soaked the ink.
Even the massive, gentle whale quivered in fear, losing its sense of direction.

Kaito clung desperately to a drifting plank, his body tossed by the furious waves.
He shouted in his heart:
"Why? How can this be?
I worked hard, I prepared,
and yet... why am I so powerless?"

At that moment, on the cliffs by the shore, a lone flame flickered in the storm.
It was Fukuda Satoshi — the Watcher. He raised the light high, his voice cutting through the wind and rain:

"Child, remember this: storms are part of the sea.
And in your career, crises never arrive with warning."

II. Storms in a Career

Fukuda's words shook Kaito to his core.
The storm was not only a natural force — it was a metaphor for life.

In careers, storms strike in many forms:

- **Economic Crises**

Global financial collapse can shatter prosperity overnight. Industries crumble, and offices once filled with light stand empty as unemployment floods the streets.

- **Company Collapse and Layoffs**

No matter your loyalty, you can lose your job in a single night. The ship you trusted may suddenly sink one morning.

- **Technological Shifts**

New technologies erase old professions without mercy. Typists fell to computers, film photographers to digital, and today AI reshapes countless industries.

- **Global Events**

Pandemics, wars, geopolitical conflicts — sudden tempests that disrupt every route across the world.

Fukuda spoke calmly:
"No one can avoid the storm.
All you can do is prepare, stay calm, and rebuild once it passes."

III. Three Principles

1. Keep Your Buoyancy
Buoyancy is the foundation of survival. Without it, no amount of struggle will save you.

In careers, buoyancy means transferable skills and resilience:
- Do you possess abilities that remain useful in any environment?
(The capacity to learn, solve problems, collaborate with others)
- Do you cultivate the calmness to endure chaos?

With buoyancy, even if an industry collapses, you can rise again.

2. Prepare a Lifeboat
A lifeboat is not luxury — it is necessity.

In careers, the lifeboat means backup options:
- Do you have savings and financial cushion?

- Do you have a network you can rely on?
- Do you have secondary skills, a side profession, or a new direction ready?

Those who gamble everything on one job stand naked before the storm. But those with a lifeboat have the space to search for new waters, even if swallowed by the waves.

3. Do Not Lose the Lighthouse
In the darkest storm, the lighthouse is your only hope.

In careers, the lighthouse is your values and long-term goals:
- Do you truly know what you want?
- Can you hold to that light, even in crisis?

Without a lighthouse, the storm swallows you whole.
With one, you can say:
"It's all right. This storm is temporary. My path still lies ahead."

IV. The Gift of the Storm

Storms do not only destroy — sometimes they bring gifts.
- One who loses a ship builds a stronger one.
- One forced from a dying industry discovers talent in another.
- One in crisis awakens hidden strength for the first time.

Fukuda said:
"The storm is the sea's exam.
It causes suffering, but it also forges growth.
The difference is not whether you encounter storms —
but whether you awaken within them."

V. Kaito's Realization

At last, the storm passed.
The clouds scattered, and light returned to the sea.

Kaito was soaked, exhausted — yet still alive.

Even more, he realized:
- He had learned to breathe steadily in chaos.
- He had found the strength to protect others.
- He had trained his eyes to seek direction in the waves.

Kaito's heart lit up.
The ocean of life could never be forever calm.
But storms were what made him into a true "man of the sea."

VI. Summary
- Storms are unavoidable — crises are part of every career.
- Three things to prepare:
Buoyancy (core skills), Lifeboat (backup options), Lighthouse (values and goals).
- Storms are both trial and gift. They awaken hidden potential.

VII. The Watcher's Final Words

Fukuda looked at Kaito, his tone gentle yet firm:

"Child, the sea will never stop its storms.
But the choice is yours:
to be swallowed by the waves,
or to become the one
who steers his course through the storm."

Kaito drew a deep breath and raised his eyes to the sky.
He knew many storms would come again — but he no longer feared them.

Because now, he had learned to sail through storms.

Chapter Eleven: Lighthouse and Sea Routes
What Kind of Person Do You Want to Become?

I. Night Sea and the Lighthouse

Night fell, and the sea turned pitch black. The wind howled, waves rolled high.
Kaito stood on the deck, surrounded by endless darkness, only the restless ocean accompanying him.

For the first time, fear crept into his heart:
"If I lose direction, if a storm strikes, will I be swallowed without a trace?"

Then, in the distance, a beam of light flickered.
It was a lighthouse, standing firm on the cliff, its beam revolving steadily through the dark.
Kaito let out a long breath of relief:
"So, even in the most dangerous times, someone always stands watch in the distance."

Fukuda Satoshi appeared at his side, his voice calm and deep:
"Kaito, you must ask yourself: in the long journey of your career, what do you wish to become?
One who depends on the lighthouse—or one who lights it?"

II. Three Types of Sailors

Fukuda lifted his hand, pointing toward the boundless sea:

"In this ocean, sailors can be divided into three types."
1. **Followers**
— They rely on the lighthouse's guidance, moving step by step.
— They lack direction of their own, but are willing to follow.
— They are safe, but never truly in control of their course.
2. **Explorers**
— Brave and unafraid, they leave the known sea routes.
— They may discover new lands—or be swallowed by hidden currents.
— They bring miracles, but also carry the risk of disaster.

3. **Lighthouse Keepers**
— They have weathered storms and understood the patterns.
— They light the way not for themselves, but for those who come after.
— They no longer chase fame or fortune, but safeguard the order of the sea.

Fukuda's tone grew firm:
"Every person shifts between these roles in a lifetime.
Kaito, you must decide—where will you ultimately stand?"

III. The Making of Sea Routes

Kaito asked with curiosity:
"But why do sea routes exist? Who decides which path people take?"

Fukuda smiled faintly:
"Sea routes are not born—they are carved by those who came before."

He spoke slowly, as if reciting memory itself:
- At the beginning, only lonely explorers ventured into the unknown. Some perished, nameless skeletons beneath the waves; others returned by fortune, bringing back a path.
- Later, some lit fires on rocky cliffs. Those flames grew into lighthouses. The light guided more sailors to repeat the same journey, until the path became a stable *route*.
- In time, the route widened. Many traveled safely upon it, forgetting the sacrifices and courage that had forged it.

"This is how careers and industries are built.
Rules are never given from the heavens. They are forged by countless trials, errors—even lives.
If you travel smoothly, it is because someone once lit a lighthouse for you."

IV. The Responsibility of the Lighthouse

Kaito thought long and deeply before asking:
"If one day I want to become a lighthouse keeper, what must I do?"

Fukuda lit an oil lamp. The flame swayed in the wind, yet it did not go out.

"To be a lighthouse keeper means three responsibilities:
      1.   **The Responsibility to Watch**
— When others are lost, you must signal them.
Not to sail for them, but to remind them of direction.
      2.   **The Responsibility to Repair**
— When a sea route is broken, you must help mend it.
Not to complain about the storm, but to ensure the path remains safe.
      3.   **The Responsibility to Pass On**
— When a new generation rises, you must give them the maps.
Not to hoard experience, but to let others go further.

Remember: a lighthouse is not merely a marker; it exists to protect."

V. Four Ways to Lose Your Way

Fukuda gazed at the restless sea, his voice solemn:
"Many never become lighthouse keepers because they lose themselves along the way."
      1.   **Lost in the Sky**
— Fixated only on lofty dreams, forgetting the foundation beneath their feet.
Dreams without roots vanish like smoke.
      2.   **Lost in the Depths**
— Obsessed with details and skills, yet blind to direction.
They are professional, yet trapped in a tiny world of their own.
      3.   **Lost in the Crowd**
— Overly dependent on others, never thinking independently.
They are safe, but forever drifting in schools of fish.
      4.   **Lost in the Unknown**
— Blindly chasing trends, without discernment.
They are bold, but often swallowed by unseen currents.

"To become a lighthouse keeper, you must avoid these forms of loss."

VI. The Parable of the Lighthouse

Fukuda fell silent for a while, then spoke with a heavy voice:

"Years ago, I visited a small harbor with an old lighthouse.
It had not been maintained—its lenses clouded, its light flickering faintly.

I warned the harbor master:
'If this continues, one day a ship will surely crash.'

But no one cared.
Some said, 'It still shines, good enough.'
Others said, 'Repairing it costs too much. Sailors can find their way by experience.'

Then came the storm.
A ship, heavy with cargo and crew, struck the reef and sank.
The cries of that night I will never forget.

Later, a stone monument was erected on the shore.
On it were carved these words:
"A lighthouse is not merely a marker; it exists to protect."

Kaito, never forget:
A lighthouse that flickers unreliably is no lighthouse at all.
Glory without responsibility cannot light the way for others.

When people rely on your light, you must ask yourself:
Will I bear their lives and hopes as my own?"

VII. Kaito's Awakening

The night deepened, stars glittering above.
Kaito stared at the lighthouse in the distance, and suddenly, the answer within him became clear.

Softly, he whispered:
"I once only wanted to swim faster, dive deeper, see sights others had never seen.
But now I understand: true value is not in how far I go,
but in whether I can become a light—guiding those who follow."

Fukuda smiled faintly, his gaze as deep as the horizon:
"Kaito, that is your final coordinate.
The ocean is vast, and your journey will one day end.

63

But the light you kindle may shine for a hundred years."

VIII. Epilogue

The waves still rolled, the sea restless.
In the distance, the lighthouse beam revolved, illuminating a safe route across the dark waters.

Kaito drew in a deep breath. For the first time, he no longer feared the unknown sea.

For he knew:
he would one day become that light—
illuminating himself, illuminating others;
safeguarding sea routes, and passing on hope.

Chapter Twelve: Direction and Destination

The Final Coordinates of Life

I. Calm After the Storm

The storm had passed, and the sea once again returned to calm.
The sky looked as though it had been washed clean, with clouds slowly drifting away in the wind.
Kaito sat alone on the deck, gazing at the endless ocean. For the first time, he felt an immense sense of vastness and solitude.

He whispered to himself:
"Storms are not the end. They are only moments that force me to see the path more clearly.
But the real question is—where am I sailing to?"

At that moment, Fukuda Satoshi stepped beside him, smiling gently:
"Child, at sea, the journey is not forever about asking 'How do I survive?'
Eventually, the question becomes—'Where do I want to go?'"

II. Three Choices of Direction

Fukuda raised his hand and pointed toward the horizon:

"When people sail upon the sea, they often face three kinds of choices."
1. **The Drifters**
— They set no destination. If the waves flow east, they drift east. If the waves push west, they drift west.
— They appear relaxed, but they will never reach a harbor of their own choosing.
2. **The Dream-Chasers**
— They set bold courses for distant horizons, chasing visions beyond the edge of sight.
— They may spend a lifetime and never arrive.
— But at least, they know why they are sailing.
3. **The Guardians of Homecoming**

— They neither drift blindly nor chase endlessly.
— They understand that the true end of a journey is homecoming, a shore that belongs to them.
— Their voyage contains both pursuit of distance and the peace of inner anchoring.

Fukuda's voice carried heavily in the wind:
"Life is not simply about conquest. It is about finding a true coordinate. The question is—what kind of person do you want to become?"

III. The Metaphor of Direction

Kaito sank into thought, visions filling his mind:
- He saw some people, like small fish, weaving endlessly in schools, living their whole lives carried by the crowd.
- He saw some people, like daring divers, exploring the wonders of the deep sea, but in the end lost in loneliness because they lacked direction.
- He saw a few, like researchers, who drew maps for all, illuminating the paths of many.
- And he saw guardians like Fukuda Satoshi, who stood silently at the shore like lighthouses, no longer sailing for themselves, but lighting the return of others.

"Direction is not merely the endpoint on a map," Kaito realized.
"It is the coordinate of the soul."

IV. The Meaning of Destination

Kaito asked Fukuda:
"Then what is destination? Is it home? Wealth? Fame?"

Fukuda shook his head with a smile:
"Destination is not just a geographic harbor. It is where your soul rests.
- Some treat destination as the accumulation of wealth.
Yet when their vaults overflow, they still feel empty.
- Some treat destination as power and status.
But once at the top, they discover that loneliness is colder than glory.
- Some treat destination as the achievement of distant dreams.

But when the dream is reached, they realize they have lost all the beauty along the way.

A true destination is this:
After you have sailed through waves, currents, and storms,
you can calmly say to yourself—
'This is the life I wanted.'"

V. Sea Lanes and Choices

Kaito remained silent for a long time.
Then he recalled all the people he had met along his journey:

- Akira, who chose safety on the beach but lost the vastness of the sea.
- Misaki, the swimmer who struggled to float yet often lost her way.
- Kenji, the diver, courageous in his exploration but burdened by solitude and danger.
- Suhua, the chart-maker, who saw the patterns of the sea but was often misunderstood.
- Fukuda Satoshi, who returned to the shore, becoming the lighthouse for others.

They had each chosen their own directions.
Some stayed on the sand.
Some wrestled with the waves.
Some plunged into the depths.
Some mapped the ocean.

And himself?
"What course should I choose?
Is it the distant dream? Or the peace of destination?
Or—can I unite both into one?"

VI. Four Types of Destinations in Life

Fukuda slowly raised four fingers:

"Child, life's destinations often take four forms."
1. **The Harbor of Material Wealth**

— Some people treat money and status as their final harbor.
They may be rich, but seldom fulfilled.
    2.   **The Island of Spirit**
— Some pursue faith, knowledge, or art, finding their home in the abundance of the soul.
They may live modestly, but within, they are rich.
    3.   **The Bay of Community**
— Some make family, friendship, or teamwork their harbor.
They find meaning in their bonds with others.
    4.   **The Lighthouse of Responsibility**
— Some ultimately become guardians. No longer sailing only for themselves, they light lamps to guide others.
Their destination is not to stop, but to protect.

Fukuda looked directly at Kaito, speaking softly:
"You must ask yourself: where is your destination?"

VII. Kaito's Awakening

Night descended, stars glittering across the sky.
Kaito lifted his head toward the heavens and suddenly understood:

"Destination is not an answer others can give me. It is the direction I must choose for myself.
Whether wealth, dreams, community, or guardianship—
as long as I choose it with my heart, that is my destination."

For the first time, a deep peace rose in his chest.
He knew that no matter how many storms awaited him, he had found his own "coordinate."

VIII. Epilogue

Fukuda Satoshi looked at the young man with quiet satisfaction:
"Child, now you understand.
Direction is not an arrow on a map, but the compass within you.
Destination is not a harbor, but the resting place of your soul."

The sea stretched endlessly.

Kaito took a deep breath, making a silent vow in his heart:

No matter how fierce the storms ahead, he would sail steadily toward his own destination.

Summary

- **Direction**: determines where you are heading.
- **Destination**: determines where your soul finds rest.
- **The wisdom of a career**: it is not about moving the fastest, but about finding the coordinates that truly belong to you.

Chapter Thirteen: Companions and Partings
Who Will Walk with You to the End?

I. Sailing at Dawn

Several days after the storm, the sea gradually regained its calm.
The light of dawn spilled across the waves, scattering in countless sparks as if stars had fallen into the water.

Kaito stood at the bow, gazing into the distance.
A thought suddenly struck him:
"If the ocean is a metaphor for my career, then what do the people around me represent?
On this voyage, who will truly walk with me until the end?"

Fukuda Satoshi heard the question, smiled gently, and spoke with a steady tone:
"Child, no matter how vast the sea, it is never entirely lonely.
There will always be companions beside you, and there will also be partings.
Some people accompany you only for a short stretch; others walk with you for a lifetime.
Learn to see this clearly, and you will not lose your way on the journey."

II. Four Types of Companions

Fukuda raised his hand and pointed in different directions:

"On the voyage of the sea, you will meet four different types of companions."
1. **Fellow Rowers**
They ride in the same boat as you.
When storms come, they row alongside you, shoulder to shoulder.
— They are your friends, teammates, and confidants, sharing both joys and sorrows with you.
Finding such people is a gift of the sea.
2. **Fellow Travelers**
They travel the same path as you for a while, but eventually they each have their own destinations.

— They may be colleagues, collaborators, or temporary partners.
When your goals align, you support each other.
But once your paths diverge, you naturally separate.

    3.   **Borrowed Riders**

They draw near to you not because they admire you, but because they wish to use you.
— They depend on you when the tide is fair, but abandon you quickly when the seas turn rough.
For such people, remain clear-eyed. Do not resent them, only recognize them.

    4.   **Opposers**

They are destined to clash with you.
— In the workplace, they may be competitors or outright obstacles.
Their presence causes pain, but also forces you to grow.

Fukuda said:
"Do not expect that everyone will stay with you until the end.
What matters most is to know who are your true fellow rowers, and who are only fellow travelers."

III. The Joy of Companionship

That day, the sea was calm and bright.
Kaito saw several small boats sailing side by side.
People on board called to one another, passed food, and even pulled each other along through waves.

His heart warmed.
"So this is the joy of having companions."

Fukuda nodded:
"Yes. Companions give you strength and courage.
The lonely may walk faster, but those with partners will always walk farther."

After a pause, he added:
"But remember, companionship requires mutual respect and understanding.
If you only wish to use others, you will eventually lose them.
True partnership is built on sincerity."

IV. The Inevitability of Partings

Not long after, Kaito witnessed another scene.
Two boats that had once sailed side by side reached a split in the current:
one was carried eastward, the other westward.

The sailors waved farewell, and their figures gradually disappeared into the horizon.

Kaito felt a pang of sorrow.
"Why must companions eventually part ways?"

Fukuda answered calmly:
"Because everyone's course is different.
Life is a constant cycle of encounters and farewells.
Some people are destined to be only passersby in your journey.
Their presence for a while is fate; their departure is inevitable.
Learn to accept partings, and you will truly cherish companionship."

V. The Meaning of Rivals

As the voyage continued, Kaito came across a boat sailing in a similar direction.
The sailors rowed swiftly, sometimes glancing at him with a challenging look.
A spark of determination rose in Kaito's heart.

"Are they the ones I must surpass?"

Fukuda laughed softly:
"Child, rivals are another gift of the sea.
Without them, you might become complacent.
Because of them, you push yourself to improve.
Remember, a rival is not an enemy but a mirror that keeps you awake."

VI. The Discipline of Solitude

One day, thick fog descended suddenly.
All the boats were separated, and Kaito found himself alone on the sea, surrounded by silence.

In that moment, he felt the weight of solitude.
"If I have no companions, can I still endure?"

Through the mist, Fukuda's voice came:
"Child, do not fear. Solitude is a training every voyager must face.
Companions can give you strength, but you cannot depend on others forever.
Only in solitude will you truly hear the voice within your own heart."

VII. Who Will Walk with You to the End?

When the fog lifted, Kaito once more saw the vast sea beneath the stars.
Suddenly he understood:
- Fellow Rowers: perhaps only one or two, but they will walk the farthest with you.
- Fellow Travelers: they bring warmth, but you must wave goodbye in the end.
- Borrowed Riders: they reveal the truth of human hearts — no need to hate, only to see clearly.
- Opposers: they force you to grow stronger.

"The ones who will truly walk with me to the end
are perhaps only the most genuine companions—
and myself."

VIII. Epilogue

The night wind brushed softly, and the sea shimmered with starlight.
Kaito whispered:
"I understand now.
On the ocean, every encounter is a gift,
and every parting is inevitable.
I cannot decide who will accompany me to the end,
but I can decide:
to cherish when we are together, and to let go when we part."

Fukuda smiled gently:
"Child, this is the truth of the sea.
Companions and partings are both parts of the journey.

You must learn to live with different people, but in the end,
you must rely on yourself to sail toward your destination."

Summary
- **Fellow Rowers**: true partners, worth treasuring most.
- **Fellow Travelers**: walk with you for a while; farewell is inevitable.
- **Borrowed Riders**: those who use you; see them clearly, no resentment needed.
- **Opposers**: competitors, the force behind your growth.

A career is like the sea.
You will never truly be alone, yet no one can walk with you forever.
Learn to be grateful in companionship, and let go in partings,
and only then will you walk farther and with greater peace.

Chapter Fourteen: Islands and Harbors
The Stopping Points Along the Journey

I. After the Drifting

The sea stretched endless, and Kaito often felt like a lone canoe adrift among the waves.
A question haunted him:
"Am I destined to drift forever? Is the ocean without end? If there are no harbors, how will I ever rest?"

One evening, as the sun sank into the horizon, a faint glow appeared in the distance.
On the line between sea and sky, the silhouette of an island emerged.
Bathed in sunset, it stood serene and still, like a silent invitation to weary sailors.

Kaito's heart leapt. He shouted:
"Sensei, land ahead! Can we finally stop and rest?"

Fukuda Satoshi smiled gently, though his gaze remained calm:
"Child, that is a harbor.
No voyage is without its stopping points.
And in every career, there are also such 'islands.'"

II. The Meaning of Islands

As the ship drew closer, the island came into focus.
Palm groves swayed, freshwater trickled, beaches glowed orange with firelight.
Travelers had gathered: some mended broken ships, some stocked provisions, others simply lay on the sand, gazing quietly at the stars.

Fukuda's voice was soft, yet firm:
"Islands and harbors carry three meanings in the ocean:
1.   **Rest** — A pause after the storm, to restore both body and spirit.
2.   **Repair** — Fixing a damaged ship, just as in work we repair gaps in our abilities.
3.   **Resupply** — Storing fresh food and water, just as we replenish with new knowledge and skills."

He paused, his tone deepened:
"If you never stop, exhaustion will consume you.
But if you cling to the harbor, you will forget the sea."

III. The Wisdom of Short Stops

Kaito stepped onto the island and felt safety return for the first time in months.
He drank from a spring, tasted fresh fruit, and felt his strength return.

"So stopping... is also part of the journey," he thought.

Fukuda looked at him and said:
"Child, short stops are so that you may travel farther.
True wisdom is not in never stopping, but in knowing when to pause—and when to sail again."

IV. Three Types of Harbors

On the sand, Fukuda traced three arcs with his finger:
"In careers, harbors take three forms."
1. **The Island of Learning**
—— This is when you pause to study and grow:
reading, training, upgrading skills.
It is like discovering new tools on the island, preparing you for the next voyage.
2. **The Harbor of Transformation**
—— Sometimes storms destroy the old ship.
In the harbor, you must build a new one.
In careers, this means changing fields, shifting roles, or redefining yourself entirely.
3. **The Harbor of Healing**
—— Long voyages wound both body and spirit.
Some take leave, others step away for a while.
It is not escape, but healing—so that you may face the sea again.

Fukuda said:
"Do not fear the harbor. Each one is a chance to depart anew."

V. The Risks of Staying

Yet harbors are not always safe.
Kaito noticed some travelers who had landed... never left.
They built huts on the sand, laid down their oars, and chose to stay forever.

"Sensei, why don't they leave?"

Fukuda sighed:
"Because they forgot the harbor is only a waystation, not the final destination.
Some stay out of fear of the storm.
Some remain out of love for comfort.
In the end, their ships rot on the beach, and their dreams decay beside them."

VI. Kaito's Dilemma

Kaito sat by a fire, staring at the sky, torn.

"I want to stay too... It's safe here. It's comfortable.
But if I never sail again, will I ever see the great ocean beyond?"

Fukuda gazed into the flames, then spoke slowly:
"Child, a true harbor is to help you rest, not to make you forget.
You must decide:
Do you stop here, or do you raise your sails once more?"

VII. Harbors Between People

On that island, Kaito met fellow travelers.
They shared food, helped one another, and told stories around the fire.

Some stories were full of failure, some brimmed with hope.
Listening, Kaito's heart stirred.
"People themselves can be harbors.
- A wise teacher lights a lamp when you're lost.
- A trustworthy partner rows beside you in solitude.
- Someone who understands you gives comfort when you're weary."
He whispered:
"So true harbors are not only on the map—they live in people's hearts."

VIII. Departure Once More

A few days later, the sea lay calm, and the horizon called.
Kaito stood at the shore, resolve clear in his eyes.

He bowed to Fukuda:
"Sensei, I've rested.
I understand now: the harbor is not where I end, but where I gather strength.
I am ready to sail again."

Fukuda smiled and nodded:
"Good.
Remember, child, the sea does not wait for those who linger.
You must learn to balance rest and journey."

IX. Epilogue

The sails filled once more, and Kaito's ship left the harbor behind.
He looked back at the island, his heart heavy with gratitude.

"Thank you for rest, thank you for strength.
But my voyage cannot end here."

Sunlight poured down, the sea shimmered, and the new journey began to unfold.

Summary

- **The meaning of harbors**: rest, repair, resupply.
- **The types of harbors**: learning, transformation, healing.
- **The risk of harbors**: comfort may make you forget the far horizon.
- **True wisdom**: stopping is not stagnation, but preparation for the next departure.

Careers are like the sea.
You must find your own stopping points—
but always remember: a harbor is not the end, but the beginning of the next chapter.

Chapter fifteen : The Stars of Navigation
How to Find Guidance in Darkness

I. The Dark Night Sea

Night fell, and the sea turned pitch black.
There was no moon, only endless darkness stretching in all directions.
The sound of the waves grew low and unfamiliar, as if whispering to the sailor:
"You are small. You might lose your way."

Kaito stood at the bow of the ship, unease rising in his heart.
In the daytime, he could rely on the sun to tell direction. But now, he could see nothing.
He whispered:
"Teacher, if the sea is completely dark, how do we move forward? Won't we be lost?"

Fukuda Satoshi lifted his head, pointing toward the sky:
"My child, look up. True guidance does not come from the sea, but from the heavens."

II. The Meaning of the Stars

When Kaito raised his eyes, he saw that the black sky was filled with countless stars.
They flickered silently, cold but clear.
Among them, one shone brightest—Polaris, the North Star—fixed firmly above, like an eternal lighthouse of the ocean.

Fukuda spoke softly:
"The ancient sailors had no compass, no maps.
How did they cross the seas?
—They relied on the stars.

The stars do not speak, but they are the most faithful friends.
They remind you: even in the darkest night, direction still exists."

Kaito felt a spark of realization:
"So in a career, the stars are vision and belief.
Without them, I would drift endlessly in the dark.
With them, I would never be lost."

III. Three Kinds of Stars

Fukuda continued:
"During long night voyages, people search for different stars.
In careers, these stars symbolize different forms of guidance."

1. **The Star of Goals — Polaris**

It always stays in the same place.
—Like one's ultimate life goal, unchanged no matter how fierce the storm.
With it, you always know where you are heading.

2. **The Stars of Stages — Constellations**

They are not permanent, but guide in different seasons.
—Like the short-term, stage-by-stage goals of a career.
For a time, you may follow one direction; once achieved, you search for the next constellation.

3. **The Stars of the Heart — The faintest lights**

They may be small, but they shine when you are most alone.
—Like a word of encouragement, a precious memory, a personal faith.
They stop you from falling into despair in the dark.

Fukuda sighed:
"Many people lose their way not because they lack ability, but because they lack stars.
No goals, no stages, no inner support—so they drift with the waves and eventually lose all direction."

IV. Stars of the Career

Kaito listened intently, and images from real life began to appear in his mind.

- Some make promotions and raises their only star.
  —This is like staring only at Polaris, forgetting the supplies needed along the way.
- Some switch paths every few years, but never hold a long-term goal.
  —This is like watching only constellations, lacking the fixed North Star.

- Some, because of a song, a phrase, or a faith, manage to endure even the hardest of times.
  —That is the starlight of the heart.

Kaito realized:
"What I need is not blind effort, but my own stars.
Only then can I keep moving forward in the darkness of the sea."

V. The Trial of Darkness

That night, a heavy fog rolled over the sea, hiding the stars.
Kaito panicked:
"Teacher, the stars are gone! What do we do now?"

But Fukuda remained calm:
"My child, the stars have never disappeared. They are only hidden.
They are still there, waiting for the fog to clear.
A true sailor does not lose faith because of temporary darkness.
They know: as long as they keep going, the stars will reappear."

Kaito fell silent. For the first time, he understood:
In a career, many times you think your goals have vanished.
But it is not that they are gone—they are only covered by fog.
What you must do is persist, not give up too soon.

VI. The Star Within

Fukuda turned and looked directly at Kaito:
"My child, remember this.
The stars in the sky wax and wane, but you must light a star within your own heart.

That star is your conviction.
—Even if everyone doubts you, you still believe.
—Even if the environment worsens, you still hold firm.
That is the most reliable lighthouse."

A surge of strength rose inside Kaito.
He whispered:
"Teacher, I understand now. The truest navigation is not only the stars above, but the star within."

VII. Epilogue

The night grew deeper, and the sea grew quiet.
Kaito lifted his gaze toward the sky, his eyes shining with determination.

He knew that the journey ahead would still hold darkness and the unknown.
But as long as there were stars—whether in the heavens or in his heart—he would never lose his way.

Fukuda smiled faintly:
"My child, this is the wisdom of navigation.
Remember: the ocean is endless, but the stars are always there.
As long as you lift your head, you will find direction."

Summary
- **The meaning of the stars**: to give direction in darkness.
- **Three types of stars**: Polaris (ultimate goal), constellations (stage-by-stage goals), faint lights (inner support).
- **The trial of darkness**: goals do not disappear; they are only hidden. Persistence reveals them again.
- **The star within**: conviction is the most reliable navigation.

Careers are like the night sea.
Only by looking up to the stars, and holding faith in your heart,
can you find your true course through the darkness.

Chapter sixteen: The Ocean and the Continent
Career Transitions and Transformation

I. The Distant Land

Kaito stood at the bow of the ship, gazing into the distance.
As dawn broke, a faint silhouette appeared on the horizon.
It was land.

A surge of excitement welled up inside him:
"Can we really make landfall?
After sailing so long across this vast, unfamiliar ocean, I finally see another world."

Fukuda Satoshi spoke softly:
"Child, what you see is the new continent.
The ocean is not the end. It is only the path that leads to the continent.
True growth is not drifting forever on the sea, but daring to cross it and set foot on new land."

Kaito felt a shock in his heart. He realized:
—This was not just a voyage,
—It was a crossing.

II. Why Cross Over?

Fukuda explained:
"Child, remember this. However vast the sea, it is not a home.
If a person only swims, dives, and studies currents, they remain forever adrift.
True transformation means becoming more than a 'man of the sea'—
It means becoming a builder on land.

This is the essence of career transitions:
—From executor to creator;
—From follower to leader;
—From a single skill to building systems and culture."

Kaito reflected deeply.
He thought of swimmers, skilled at floating but never leaving the surface.
He thought of divers, harvesting treasures but unable to bring them back to land.
He thought of researchers, mapping the ocean yet still confined to their ships.

"The key is not just knowing how to sail, but daring to land."

III. The Fear of Landing

But as the ship drew closer to the shore, Kaito felt unease.
The continent was strange and barren, hiding unknown reefs or dangers.

He whispered:
"Teacher, what if I land and find it doesn't suit me?
What if I lose the safety of the sea?"

Fukuda smiled and shook his head:
"This is why most people never dare to cross.
They would rather drift at sea forever than risk the shore.
But you must understand:
Even the strongest ship is only temporary shelter.
Only land can give you roots and a home."

Kaito fell silent.
He realized career transitions always come with fear and uncertainty.
Yet if he remained in familiar waters, he would never reach new heights.

IV. Three Stages of Crossing

Fukuda pointed toward the land:
1. **Seeing the Land — Recognizing the Need to Change**
—Many stay at sea simply because they don't know land exists.
—Only when you realize your current role or industry cannot sustain the future do you begin to seek new ground.
2. **Reaching Shore — Preparation and Testing**
—Landing is not a blind leap. It requires preparation: skills, resources, networks.
—You must find safe entry points, avoiding reefs and waves.

3. **Taking Root — Building on the New Continent**
—True transition is not a brief landing but the ability to stay.
—It means adapting to new rules, creating new values, producing new outcomes.

Kaito nodded slowly.
Crossing over was not impulse, but foresight and courage combined.

V. The Challenge of New Land

When the ship finally anchored, Kaito stepped onto the unfamiliar shore.
It was not the paradise he imagined—mud, jungle, thorns, and strange noises surrounded him.

He sighed:
"So, landing doesn't mean safety. It's another challenge."

Fukuda nodded:
"Yes. The ocean taught you how to sail.
But the continent forces you to learn how to survive and build.
You must carve paths, build shelter, and cooperate with other settlers.

This is the essence of career transition:
—From adapting to the sea, to creating on land."

VI. The Fates of Different Settlers

On land, Kaito met several kinds of people:
1. **Pioneers**
—They swung axes, clearing jungle and opening paths.
—In careers, they are entrepreneurs who start from zero.
2. **Builders**
—They erected houses and formed settlements.
—In careers, they are managers, integrating scattered resources into systems.
3. **The Lost**
—Frightened by strangeness, they quickly retreated back to the sea.

—In careers, they are those who attempt change but return to the comfort zone.

Fukuda sighed:
"Not everyone succeeds in crossing.
But only those who persist in exploration truly take root and claim the new land."

VII. Kaito's Dilemma

As night fell, the new continent was strange and chaotic.
Kaito felt torn:
—He missed the sea's familiarity,
—Yet was drawn to the land's unknown promise.

He looked at Fukuda and asked:
"Teacher, how should I choose?
Return to the sea, or stay here to build my world?"

Fukuda's eyes were steady:
"Kaito, the sea and the continent are not opposites.
You must know how to sail the ocean,
But you must also learn to build on land.
A true career is neither endless drifting nor fixed roots alone.
It is moving freely between sea and land."

VIII. The Wisdom Behind Crossing

Raising his lamp, Fukuda said firmly:
"Remember, child. The wisdom of crossing has three parts:
1. **Keep Learning** — No one is born fit for new land. Learning is the only weapon.
2. **Stay Resilient** — Landing always brings setbacks. Only persistence takes root.
3. **Carry Value** — If you can bring your ocean experience to the land, you will have a true advantage."

Kaito nodded slowly. Strength rose in his heart.

IX. Epilogue

At dawn, sunlight spread across the new continent.
Kaito shouldered his pack, joining pioneers as they marched into the jungle.
He knew the path ahead bristled with thorns, but also infinite possibility.

He whispered to himself:
"I will cross over. I will no longer be just a traveler at sea.
I will build my future on land."

In the distance, Fukuda smiled, watching him vanish into the new world.

Summary

- **The Ocean**: Symbol of drifting, exploration, and learning.
- **The Continent**: Symbol of transformation, construction, and rooting.
- **Three Stages of Crossing**: Seeing the land, approaching shore, taking root.
- **Different Settlers**: Pioneers, builders, the lost.
- **Wisdom of Crossing**: Learning, resilience, transferring value.

A career is not endless drifting on the ocean,
nor permanent stagnation on the continent.
It is a **crossing**.
Only those who dare to land
can truly discover a new world.

Chapter Seventeen: Companions of the Voyage
The Power of Cooperation and Teamwork

I. The Lonely Voyager

After landing on the new continent, Kaidō often wandered alone at its edges.
He chopped trees in the forest, tried to set up tents by himself,
yet he soon realized:
no matter how hard one tries, it is difficult for a single person to truly open up a world of his own.

By the campfire at night, he whispered to Fukuda Satoshi:
"Teacher, I've come so far, but I feel more and more lonely.
I miss the sea, yet the land feels so unfamiliar.
Is the real path something I must walk alone?"

Fukuda gazed at the flames and slowly shook his head:
"Child, the journeys across sea and land were never meant to be solitary.
A ship rowed by one person will soon stand still.
Only by finding companions can you sail toward a farther future."

II. The Meaning of Companions

Fukuda picked up a piece of wood and threw it into the fire.
The flames immediately grew brighter.

"Do you see?
A single piece of wood burns only so long,
but when joined with others, it lights up the entire night.
So it is with one's career.
An individual's talent is limited, but together, a team creates far greater value."

He went on:
"In the ocean of work and life, there are three kinds of companions:
1. **Fellow Rowers** — those who row alongside you and share the battles;

2.   **Guiding Mentors** — those who shine like lighthouses and show you the way;

3.   **Future Followers** — those who grow under the light you kindle.

When you have companions, guidance, and the ability to lead others,
you are no longer just a lone voyager — you are a true navigator."

III. Different Types of Companions

1. Oar Companions

Some travel right beside you, like oar companions.
They row through the storm with you, shoulder to shoulder.
— In the workplace, they are your colleagues who share the tasks.

Kaidō remembered meeting a swimmer at sea.
Though their directions were not always the same,
they once supported each other in a gale and made it back to shore together.
He realized for the first time: joint strength is far more effective than solitary struggle.

2. Lighthouse Mentors

Others may not be on your boat, yet they shine a light from afar.
When you lose your way, their beam helps you recover your course.
— In careers, they are mentors, guides, and transmitters of wisdom.

Fukuda smiled:
"Like I am to you. I do not row your boat,
but I remind you: reefs lie ahead, currents flow here.
The mentor's value is not to walk for you, but to make your walking clearer."

3. New Followers

Fukuda looked firmly at Kaidō:
"One day, you too will be a lighthouse for others.
Young people will seek your guidance;
some in storms will need your help.
When you can light the way for others,
you will finally understand the true meaning of companions."

IV. The Trial of Companionship

But companions are not always perfect.
On the new land, Kaidō saw:

- Some sought only to take advantage, but gave nothing in return.
- Some appeared cooperative, yet hid rivalry behind their smiles.
- Some were passionate at first, then abandoned the effort halfway.

He felt confused, even disheartened.

"Teacher, if companions may betray or abandon me, how can I rely on them?"

Fukuda's gaze was steady:
"Child, you must learn to discern.
— Who is a true companion, and who is just a passerby.
True companions stand with you in storms, not only in calm seas.
Remember, companionship is not about numbers, but about depth."

V. Building a Team

One day, Kaidō met others who had also landed.
Some could build huts, others could hunt, and some could draw maps.
At first, each worked alone, and efficiency was low.
Then, when another storm struck, they realized cooperation was necessary.

Kaidō proposed:
"Let's divide tasks.
Some build shelters, some search for food, some chart the routes.
Only then can we survive on this land."

From that moment, a small team was formed.
Efficiency rose, safety grew, and trust began to take root.

From afar, Fukuda watched with quiet satisfaction, murmuring:
"He finally understands — teamwork is the key to crossing oceans and rooting on land."

VI. The Power of Companionship and Teamwork

Kaidō gradually learned:
- One person's knowledge is limited, but a team's knowledge can complement each other.
- One person's strength is limited, but a team's strength can resist the storm.
- One person's dream is limited, but a team's dream can transform the world around them.

In a career, a team is the most important vessel.
With a team, you evolve from a swimmer to a sailor, from a diver to a builder.

VII. The Fire and the Spirit of Teamwork

One night, the campfire was about to die.
Everyone was exhausted; no one wanted to gather more wood.
Kaidō stood up and threw in his last bit of strength.

He whispered:
"If the fire dies, we will all shrink in the dark.
But as long as the flames burn, we can keep each other warm."

This act stirred everyone's hearts.
They all rose, adding wood to the fire.
The flames roared, warming the whole team.

Fukuda's eyes glimmered as he spoke softly:
"This is the power of leadership.
One person willing to go further inspires everyone else.
Companions are not born, teams are not born —
they are ignited."

VIII. Kaidō's Awakening

After countless rounds of cooperation and trial, Kaidō finally understood:
The true value of a career is not only in personal growth,
but in whether you can build a community of voyagers with companions.

Looking at his teammates, his heart grew resolute:
"I am no longer just a sailor.
I will become the one who ignites the team.
For only a team can sail across wider seas and reach farther lands."

Summary
- **The meaning of companions**: fuel for the fire, oars for the ship.
- **Three types of companions**: fellow voyagers, mentors, and followers.
- **The trial of companionship**: distinguish true partners from passersby.
- **The power of teamwork**: knowledge complement, strength multiplied, dreams extended.
- **The essence of leadership**: to ignite others, even if you must give first.

The sea of careers is not a lonely drift,
but a voyage shared with companions.
Only when you learn to find partners, build teams, and inspire others
can you truly become a navigator.

Chapter Eighteen : Lighthouse and Voyage
Leadership and Legacy

I. The Lighthouse in the Night

That night, Kaito walked alone to the shore.
The horizon was pitch black, the sound of crashing waves like endless drums.
Yet in the deepest darkness, he saw a faint glow — a lighthouse on the coast.

It was a flame lit by Fukuda Satoshi himself.
The oil lamp swayed in the wind and rain, but it never went out.
It was like an eye, watching over the vast darkness, guiding the lost at sea.

Kaito's heart trembled:
"True leadership is not about walking in front,
but about lighting a lamp so that those who come after know where to go."

II. Fukuda's Memory

Standing by the lighthouse, Fukuda said slowly to Kaito:

"When I was young, I was just like you, filled with dreams, and I leapt into the sea.
I swam furiously, I dived deep, I even drew maps of the currents.
But later I realized, no matter how far I traveled, there were always people losing their way.

So I chose to return to the shore,
to watch over them, to remind them, to keep this light burning.
This lamp is not just for me — it is for everyone out at sea."

He paused, his tone solemn:
"Child, understand this: leadership is not control.
Leadership is illumination."

III. The Meaning of the Lighthouse

Fukuda raised the lamp and said to Kaito:

"A lighthouse has three meanings:

1.   **To guide the lost**

Like a senior in an industry, it warns the newcomer:

'There are shallows there, don't go.

There is a current there, you can use it.'

2.   **To give hope in storms**

When the night is darkest and the storm fiercest,

the lighthouse whispers: 'You are not utterly lost. There is still light.'

3.   **To leave a legacy**

The lighthouse is not only for the present.

It burns from generation to generation,

so that even those who never knew the one who lit it

can still find their way forward."

Kaito stared at the lamp, his chest burning with heat.

At last he understood: the value of leadership is not how many you take with you,

but how much light you leave behind.

IV. The Training of Leadership

Kaito asked:

"Teacher, how can I become a true leader?"

Fukuda smiled and answered:

"The training of leadership has four stages:

1.   **Ignite yourself first**

— If you have no flame, how can you light others?

Find your inner fire: vision, conviction, values.

2.   **Learn to light others**

— Leadership is not about shining alone, but making others shine.

When you share experience and trust, others will be ignited.

3.   **Stand firm in the darkness**

— A true leader does not appear only when the sea is calm,

but when storms rage and others retreat, you must remain lit.

4.   **Leave sparks behind**

— One day you will depart.

If you leave fire behind,

others can continue to light the lamp,

and your leadership will not disappear."

V. The Call of the Voyage

One day, the team decided:
They would not remain on the new continent forever.
They wanted to sail again, to seek wider horizons.

The younger ones were thrilled, but also anxious.
Some asked:
"What if we lose our way?"
"What if storms strike again?"

Fukuda placed the lamp in Kaito's hands:
"From today, this light belongs to you.
I will remain on the shore, but the voyage ahead must be completed by you.
Carry this lamp, and let them know: even in darkness, there is light."

Kaito held the lamp with both hands, his heart heavy.
It was both a burden and a mission.

VI. Kaito's First Lighting

The voyage began.
And indeed, a storm arose.
Clouds swallowed the sky, waves battered the ship, people panicked.

In the chaos, Kaito raised the lamp.
The flame wavered, yet it pierced the storm, reflecting in everyone's eyes.

"Do not fear! We have light!"

With him at the helm, the crew steadied themselves.
When the storm passed, they realized with awe:
the lamp had not only shown direction,
it had lit courage in every heart.

VII. The Meaning of Legacy

Kaito finally understood why Fukuda had chosen to remain a Watcher.
Watching was not retreat — it was ensuring that others had the strength to go on.

He whispered to himself:
"One day, I too will be like my teacher.
I will pass this lamp into the hands of the next."

For leadership is not measured by how many followers you command,
but by how many, under your light,
learn to light their own lamps.

VIII. Kaito's Awakening

That night, the stars glittered, and the sea lay still.
Kaito stood at the bow, holding the lamp, gazing toward the horizon.

He was no longer the confused youth,
no longer just a swimmer, a diver, or even a mapmaker.

He had become a **keeper of the lighthouse flame**,
a leader of voyages,
a bearer of legacy.

Summary

- **The Lighthouse's Meaning**: Guidance, hope, and legacy.
- **The Training of Leadership**: Ignite yourself, ignite others, stand firm in darkness, leave sparks behind.
- **The Essence of Leadership**: Not control, but illumination.
- **The Value of Legacy**: To pass light from generation to generation, so others may find their way in darkness.

The sea of a career will one day demand this of you:
to move from being one who is guided,
to becoming one who lights the lamp.

Only then will you complete the transformation
from traveler to navigator,
from voyager to leader.

Chapter Nineteen : The Ultimate Trial of Sailing

Solitude and Freedom

1. The End of the Sea

After months of voyaging, Kaito's ship finally sailed into a vast and unfamiliar sea.
There were no islands, no markers, and not a single shadow of another vessel.
Only the endless blank where sky and sea intertwined, as though he had reached the edge of the world.

Night fell. The wind stilled, the waves calmed.
The crew slept soundly, leaving Kaito alone at the bow.
Gazing at the stars above, he felt something he had never known before:
solitude.

This solitude was not mere loneliness,
but a deep, hollow emptiness,
as though the entire sea whispered to him:
"Here, there is only you."

2. Fukuda's Echo

In the silence of night, Kaito seemed to hear Fukuda Satoshi's voice once again:

"Child, remember, the ultimate trial of the sea is not storms, nor currents.
It is whether you can live with solitude."

Kaito whispered to the sky:
"Teacher, I understand.
Storms terrify me, currents disorient me, whirlpools make me struggle—
but solitude... solitude makes me question the meaning of my existence."

3. The Three Realms of Solitude

In the darkness, Kaito reflected and slowly understood the three realms of solitude:

1.   **Physical solitude**
— When you face the vast sea alone, no one can row for you.
Just as in the early stages of a career, you must complete your work independently; no one can replace you.

2.   **Spiritual solitude**
— Even when surrounded by others, there are times no one truly understands you.
When you go deeper and farther than the rest, that feeling of "no resonance" is spiritual solitude.

3.   **Existential solitude**
— When you reach a new height and see vistas unseen by others, you begin to question:
"Why am I here? Where am I headed?"
This pursuit of meaning is the deepest solitude of all.

4. The Price of Freedom

Yet within solitude, Kaito gradually discovered another force—**freedom**.

He realized:
In this boundless sea, no one could restrain him, no one could command him.
Direction was his choice; the route, his to chart.

Solitude is painful, but freedom is magnificent.
The two are inseparable:
If you fear solitude, you will never truly know freedom.
If you pursue freedom, you must learn to endure solitude.

5. A Dialogue in Solitude

Kaito closed his eyes and seemed to converse with his own heart:

Inner voice:
"Why continue sailing?

You already have companions, a lighthouse—why risk venturing further into the unknown?"

Kaito's reply:
"Because the sea has no end.
If I stop now, I will lose true freedom.
Even if ahead lies only solitude, I must see it for myself."

6. The Return of Companionship

At dawn, sunlight spread across the deck.
The crew awoke and saw Kaito still standing at the bow.

"Captain, you didn't sleep all night? What were you thinking about?"

Kaito smiled:
"I was thinking about why we are here.
I finally understand: solitude is not the enemy—it is a path to growth.
But even so, I am grateful—
we are not sailing alone."

The crew fell silent.
They realized:
Because Kaito could face solitude alone, he could lead them toward freedom.

7. The Balance of Solitude and Freedom

Kaito drew his own truth:
- Fear solitude, and you will forever depend on the crowd, losing freedom.
- Chase only freedom, and you may fall into isolation, losing support.
- True wisdom lies in balancing solitude with freedom.

He resolved:
To guard his companions, yet also dare to walk alone;
To embrace freedom, yet also accept responsibility.

8. The Ultimate Test of a Career

Fukuda's words echoed again:

"Child, the ultimate test of a career is not how much money you earn,
nor how far you travel.
It is whether, in solitude, you can remain steadfast;
and in freedom, whether you can bear responsibility.

Solitude makes you yourself.
Freedom lets you shape the future.
Only those who can hold both solitude and freedom
are true voyagers."

9. Kaito's Awakening

Kaito stood at the bow, arms wide open to embrace the infinite sea.
The wind brushed his face—he no longer felt fear.

At last, he understood:
The sea would not give him answers.
The answer was within himself.

Solitude is not the end.
Freedom is the destination.
And the true value of freedom
is choosing to move forward, even in solitude.

10. Summary
   - The three realms of solitude: physical, spiritual, existential.
   - The essence of freedom: choosing your own path, free from external control.
   - Wisdom of balance: solitude is the price of freedom, freedom is the sublimation of solitude.
   - The ultimate test: remaining steadfast in solitude, bearing responsibility in freedom.

The ocean of a career is not about others rowing for you.
It is whether, between solitude and freedom,
you can find your own **ultimate course**.

Chapter Twenty : Homecoming and Rebirth

After You Have Crossed the Sea

I. Looking Back on the Voyage

On a calm morning, Haito stood at the bow of his ship.
In the distance, a faint outline of land emerged.
His heart trembled — it was the signal of homecoming.

He looked back at the vast sea:
- He had once been a confused youth, standing on the shore, afraid to step into the water;
- He had once been a swimmer, drifting with the surface currents;
- He had once been a diver, exploring the wonders of the deep, tasting both solitude and danger;
- He had once followed the researchers, drawing sea charts, learning the rules of the ocean;
- He had once stood beneath Fukuda Satoshi's lighthouse, learning what it meant to guard and to pass on.

Now, he had completed a full voyage.
But he knew in his heart: this was not the end, but another kind of beginning.

II. The Meaning of Homecoming

Haito pondered:
"Why do people return home? Why not keep sailing forever?"

Gradually, he understood — homecoming has three layers of meaning:
1. **Sorting and Reflection**
The experiences of a voyage must be settled during the return.
If you only sail forward without looking back, you will lose yourself.
2. **Sharing and Passing On**
Homecoming is to bring experience back to shore, to tell those who follow:
"There is a current there, there are reefs there."
It is the transmission of knowledge and wisdom.

3.   A New Departure
Homecoming is not stagnation, but replenishment.
Only by returning to shore can you repair your ship, restock supplies, and prepare for the next, longer voyage.

III. Encounter at the Shore

As the ship drew near land, an old man with white hair stood at the shore.
It was Fukuda.

He had long been waiting there, as if he knew Haito would one day return.
Their eyes met, and Haito was overwhelmed with tears.

"Teacher, I am back."
Fukuda smiled and patted his shoulder:
"Good. And what have you brought back?"

Haito paused, then replied:
"I have brought back solitude, but also freedom.
I have brought back responsibility, but also hope.
Most importantly — I have brought back myself."

IV. The Flame of Sharing

On the shore gathered many young people.
Their eyes were just like Haito's long ago — curious, confused, and tinged with hesitation.

They asked:
"Did you really see the world beneath the sea?"
"How terrifying are the storms?"
"What does freedom feel like?"

Haito smiled and patiently shared his journey:
- The struggles when first entering the sea;
- The awe and danger of diving deep;
- The fear and growth in storms;
- The reflection and awakening in solitude.

He did not boast, but told the truth plainly:

"The sea is beautiful, but also cruel.
Only those who are prepared can go farther.
But remember this: no matter how much you long for the horizon, the lighthouse is always behind you."

The young listened intently, and their eyes grew brighter.
In that moment, Haito realized: he too was becoming a **guardian**.

V. Rebirth of the Homecoming

Homecoming is not only sharing, but rebirth.
On land, Haito rested and repaired his ship.
He discovered he was no longer as impatient as before.
- He had learned patience — for when the wind is wrong, the voyage will fail.
- He had learned choice — not every route is worth the risk.
- He had learned inheritance — passing experience to those who follow is more meaningful than sailing alone.

He understood:
Homecoming is not an ending, but a rebirth of the soul.
Only those who have crossed the sea truly understand the value of the shore.

VI. A New Calling

One evening, Haito walked alone to the shore.
Far on the horizon, new stars were flickering.
He knew — it was the call of the next voyage.

He whispered:
"I am no longer who I once was.
This time, I will not only seek freedom.
I will light the way for others."

He decided: he would no longer voyage alone, but lead a team.
This time, his ship would not belong only to himself,
but to all who yearned for the horizon.

VII. Fukuda's Blessing

Before departure, Fukuda placed the lamp into Haito's hands and repeated the familiar words:

"Child, the sea will never cease its storms,
nor will it cease its beauty.
Take this lamp,
so that those who come after will know — even in the dark, there is light."

Haito nodded, his gaze resolute:
"Teacher, I will.
Wherever I go, I will remember:
I am not only a sailor, but also a guardian."

VIII. The Fable's Closing

The sea is like a career:
- Everyone must depart from the shore;
- Everyone will face storms and solitude;
- Everyone must find their own coordinates and lighthouse.

Homecoming is not the end,
but the chance to carry back experience, responsibility, and conviction,
and then set out again toward a greater freedom.

Summary
- **Meaning of homecoming**: reflection, sharing, replenishment.
- **Value of homecoming**: inheritance of experience, inspiring others.
- **Essence of rebirth**: no longer drifting only for oneself, but shining for others.
- **The new call**: after homecoming, another voyage awaits.

The fable of career tells us:
When you have crossed the sea,
what you bring back is not only success and failure,
but growth, responsibility, and the flame that lights the voyage of others.

Chapter Twenty one : The Sea and the Stars
The Ultimate Meaning of Career

I. The Meeting of Sea and Stars

The night was deep. The sea stretched out like a vast black mirror, reflecting the stars above.
Kaito stood alone at the bow, gazing at the heavens, hearing nothing but the waves striking the hull.

Suddenly, he remembered something Fukuda Satoshi once said:

**"Child, the sea teaches you how to survive.
The stars tell you why you live."**

In that moment, he understood:
The sea symbolizes career — the skills and journeys of survival.
The stars symbolize values — the meaning and direction of life.
They complement each other. Neither can be missing.

II. The Teachings of the Sea

Looking back on his voyage, Kaito began to see the threefold lessons of the sea:
1. **The sea is a classroom of survival**
It teaches you how to breathe, how to swim, how not to sink in storms.
Just as a career teaches you how to feed yourself and stay afloat in competition.
2. **The sea is a furnace of growth**
It forces you to face fear, strengthens your endurance, pushes you past your limits.
Just as challenges and failures in work force you to grow.
3. **The sea is an arena of responsibility**
When you no longer swim only for yourself, but to guide and guard others, you become a true "voyager" in your profession.

III. The Call of the Stars

But the sea alone cannot sustain a voyage.
Without the stars, a ship merely drifts.

The stars remind Kaito:
- Career is not the destination, only the means.
- Values are the direction, answering the question "why go at all?"

The stars embody three layers of meaning:
1. **Vision** — The faraway place you long to reach, not salary, but mission.
2. **Belief** — The strength that keeps you afloat when storms strike.
3. **Legacy** — When you leave, whether you can pass on the light and the route to those who follow.

IV. A Dialogue Between Sea and Stars

One dawn, Kaito closed his eyes and seemed to hear the sea and the stars in conversation.

The sea said:
"I am reality, survival, the challenge you must face."

The stars said:
"I am ideals, meaning, the light that keeps you from being lost in the dark."

The sea said:
"Without me, you cannot live."

The stars said:
"Without me, you do not know why you live."

Kaito opened his eyes and sighed deeply:
"So career and life are like the sea and the stars.
One teaches me how to live.
The other teaches me why to live."

V. The Ultimate Meaning of Career

Kaito finally understood:
The ultimate meaning of a career is not position or wealth.
It is finding your own values and mission through what you do.

- Some choose to be lighthouses, guarding others.
- Some choose to be divers, exploring the depths.
- Some choose to be researchers, drawing charts.
- Some choose to be Watchers, passing on experience.

Whatever the role, as long as it helps you see the stars and light the way for others,
your career is no longer just survival — it becomes a voyage of life.

VI. Kaito's Awakening

One night, Kaito lifted the lamp of inheritance and gazed at the brightest star in the sky.
He made a silent vow:

"I will make my career not just a way to feed myself,
but a light for others, a watch for the world.

I will make my voyage
not just drifting on the sea,
but a great sailing under the stars."

At last, he understood the meaning of Fukuda's lifelong watch.
It was not retreat — it was the deepest freedom.

VII. Epilogue

Dawn broke, sunlight spilled, and the sea glittered gold.
Kaito, with his companions, set sail once more.
The lighthouse's flame still shone behind, the stars still guided ahead.

The voyage of career continued,
but he was no longer lost.

For he knew:

- **The sea teaches him how to face reality.**
- **The stars tell him the meaning of life.**

This is the ultimate answer of career:
Survival and meaning, action and value,
the sea and the stars — both are indispensable.

Conclusion: Becoming an Ocean Watcher

The ocean is boundless, and the waves never cease.
Some remain on the shore, watching from a distance.
Some swim on the surface, carried by the tide.
Some dive into the deep, bearing pressure and solitude.
Some chart maps to understand the currents.
And some, at last, light the flame—becoming Ocean Watchers.

Isn't a career much the same?
- You may still be on the shore, hesitant to take your first step.
- You may be swimming hard every day, yet unsure of your direction.
- You may be diving deep, immersed in expertise, but surrounded by loneliness.
- You may be charting the sea, seeking to understand the whole landscape of your field.
- Or you may already be watching—guiding others with wisdom and experience.

Each stage carries meaning. None is higher or lower than the other.
The question is: Do you know where you are?
And are you willing to go further?

Three Lessons of the Ocean

1. **Facing the Environment**

The ocean teaches us: currents and undercurrents are stronger than any individual.
So too in a career—trends and environments shape the larger path.
Learn to read them, and you will not struggle in vain.

2. **Facing Yourself**

The deep holds not only wonders, but darkness and fear.
In your career, you must face not only external challenges,
but also your own fragility and desires.
Only by reconciling with yourself can you keep sailing.

3. **Facing Others**

The ocean teems with fish, sharks, whales, turtles, and coral.
You cannot choose to be alone forever.
You must learn to coexist, to navigate relationships.
And ultimately, ask yourself: Who will you be in this ocean?

Watching and Guiding

Watching is not withdrawal—it is transcendence.
The Ocean Watcher has seen the storms, felt the undercurrents,
and learned the complexity of human nature.
They choose not only to journey for themselves,
but also to stand as a lighthouse—guiding and guarding others.

As Fukuda once said:
"Child, the ocean never stops, and neither does the journey of work.
You must find rhythm in the waves,
bear pressure in the deep,
and hold steady in the storm.
At last, you will become the light—
illuminating others, and illuminating yourself."

Stars and Land

If the ocean represents career,
then the stars represent meaning,
and the land represents homecoming.

The ocean teaches you how to survive.
The stars remind you why you live.
The land gives you a place to create and rest.

Only when you understand the ocean, the stars, and the land together
will your journey be complete.

An Ocean Watcher does not conquer the sea.
They understand it, live with it, and pass on its wisdom.
They look up to the stars, stand on solid ground,
yet their heart always belongs to the endless ocean.

Questions for the Reader
- Where are you in the ocean right now?
- How do you sense the currents and undercurrents?
- Around you, who are the fish, the sharks, the whales, and the coral?
- When the storm comes, where is your buoyancy, your lifeboat, your lighthouse?

- Which star and which shore are waiting for you in the distance?

When you can answer these questions,
you have already begun the path of becoming an Ocean Watcher.

Final Words

A career is not a straight line—it is a vast ocean.
You cannot decide when the waves will rise,
but you can choose your stance.
You cannot command when the stars will shine,
but you can choose to lift your eyes.
You cannot bring the shore closer,
but you can prepare the courage to land.

May you, in the great ocean of life,
find your place,
sail under the stars,
rest upon the land,
and ultimately become—

An Ocean Watcher.

Reader's Guide — Your Navigation Manual

Each chapter has three parts:
- **Chapter Summary** : the key metaphor and main learning points.
- **Reflection Question** : prompts for self-reflection, linking ideas to your own career.
- **Action Suggestion** : small, practical steps to help you put insights into action.

Chapter 1 ◖ Opening Parable

Summary: The ocean represents a career—vast, risky, yet full of possibilities. Everyone must ask: *"Where am I in this ocean?"*

Reflection: Do you see your career as just a job, or as a voyage?

Action: Use a natural metaphor to describe your current career state.

Chapter 2 ◖ The One Standing on the Beach

Summary: Observing, hesitant to enter, staying at the career's edge.

Reflection: Are you still standing on the shore, afraid to begin?

Action: Set one small challenge to step outside your comfort zone.

Chapter 3 ◖ The Swimmer

Summary: Already in the water but easily drifting, lacking direction.

Reflection: Are you truly moving forward, or just drifting?

Action: Track one week of work and see how much aligns with long-term goals.

Chapter 4 The Diver

Summary: Skilled, willing to go deep, but facing loneliness and risk.
  Reflection: Do you have enough "equipment" to support your deep dive?
  Action: Identify three skills to strengthen, and make a learning plan.

Chapter 5 The Ocean Researcher

Summary: Understands patterns, predicts trends, sees the big picture.
  Reflection: Are you only executing tasks, or also understanding the system?
  Action: Start an "industry observation journal" and update it monthly.

Chapter 6 The Practitioner: Becoming a Watcher

Summary: Applies learning, lights the way for others, takes on responsibility.
  Reflection: Are you willing to be a small lighthouse for someone else?
  Action: Share one experience to guide a newcomer or colleague.

Chapter 7 Your Above, Below, Left, and Right

Summary: Sky = goals, seabed = roots, peers = relationships, unknown = opportunities.
  Reflection: Do your "sky and seabed" (goals and values) align?
  Action: Draw your personal "career compass map."

Chapter 8 Currents and Undercurrents

Summary: Trends, culture, and storms shape careers.
  Reflection: Which current is pushing you right now?
  Action: Follow one industry trend and think about its impact on you.

Chapter 9 Creatures of the Ocean

Summary: Fish, sharks, whales, turtles, coral reefs, impostors—different roles in the workplace.

Reflection: Which "creatures" are around you?

Action: Observe three people around you and identify their "type."

Chapter 10 Storms and Accidents

Summary: Crises, reefs, and fog are unavoidable tests.

Reflection: Do you have your own "lifeboat"?

Action: Create a "career crisis checklist" with risks and responses.

Chapter 11 Lighthouses and Routes

Summary: Lighthouse = values, route = choices.

Reflection: Where is your lighthouse?

Action: Write one sentence that captures your core value.

Chapter 12 Direction and Destination

Summary: Three types of destinations: material, spiritual, legacy.

Reflection: Which one do you truly desire?

Action: Write a letter "to yourself in 10 years."

Chapter 13 Companions and Departures

Summary: Some walk with you for a while, some for a lifetime.

Reflection: Who are your true companions?

Action: Express gratitude to someone you want to keep in your journey.

Chapter 14 🌙 Islands and Harbors

Summary: Rest, repair, and resupply—career pit stops, but not the final destination.
🌑 Reflection: Have you stayed in a harbor too long, forgetting to set sail again?
✳️ Action: Plan one "rest stop" to restore yourself before your next move.

Chapter 15 🌙 The Stars of Navigation

Summary: North Star = ultimate goal; constellations = milestones; starlight = inner support.
🌑 Reflection: What is your "North Star"?
✳️ Action: Write down three milestone goals with deadlines.

Chapter 16 🌙 The Ocean and the Continent

Summary: Moving between drifting and stability—career transitions.
🌑 Reflection: Do you need to step onto new land?
✳️ Action: Evaluate one possible transition path, and identify the first step.

Chapter 17 🌙 Companions of the Voyage

Summary: The strength of teams determines survival and progress.
🌑 Reflection: Which type of partner do you lack most?
✳️ Action: Actively build or strengthen one relationship.

Chapter 18 🌙 Lighthouses and Long Voyages

Summary: Leadership is to illuminate, not control; legacy is to leave fire behind.
🌑 Reflection: What kind of light do you want to leave behind?
✳️ Action: Lead one small team task and reflect on it.

Chapter 19 ☾ The Ultimate Test of Sailing

Summary: Loneliness is the price of freedom; freedom is the elevation of loneliness.
- Reflection: Can you truly accept loneliness?
- Action: Spend one day alone and record your feelings.

Chapter 20 ☾ Return and Renewal

Summary: Returning is not the end—it means reflection, sharing, and rebirth.
- Reflection: How will you share your flame with others?
- Action: Write a reflection piece and share it with friends or colleagues.

Chapter 21 ☾ The Ocean and the Stars

Summary: The ocean = reality and survival; the stars = values and direction. Both are essential.
- Reflection: Are you only following the ocean, or also gazing at the stars?
- Action: Spend 5 minutes daily asking: "Are my actions moving me closer to my star?"

Conclusion ☾ ✦ Becoming a Watcher of the Ocean and the Stars
- A career is not a straight line but an ocean voyage.
- The ocean teaches survival; the stars reveal meaning.
- May you ultimately become a **Watcher of the Ocean and the Stars**.

www.ingramcontent.com/pod-product-compliance
Lightning Source LLC
Chambersburg PA
CBHW081139090426

42736CB00018B/3412